STEP BY STEP
DRAWING
FOREST
ANIMALS
for kids
I0788478
Miriam R. Ahumada

Little
Pencil

CONTENTS

STEP BY STEP

Copyrights 2020 Little Pencil

Published by: Little Pencil

hello@littlepencilpress.com

ABOUT THE AUTHOR

Miriam R. Ahumada

is a young illustrator that loves to draw and sing. Singing is a dream she still has time to pursue.

Miriam started drawing as a three year old thanks to his father and his T.V preferences, yeah she liked watching the one, and only Bob Ross draw happy trees. Then when she was a little bit older, her inspiration became her cousin and her aunt Teresa, who showed her a lot of their own art when they were her age. Eventually she discovered Loish and decided to dive into digital art.

Miriam gathers inspiration from a lot of places and people like her own friends and other artists. She hopes that looking into this book as easy or difficult this drawing may seem,

you get the inspiration to create your own art and explore all you can do!

This is to Quinni art, whose art inspired and continues to inspire me wherever she is.

INTRODUCTION

Ever dreamed of putting that image in your head on paper?

Ever tried to describe something so detailed that only a picture or image could do it justice?

I think almost everyone at least one time in their lives tried, failed, and gave up on drawing. The idea of it it's so much fun! Creating something from your imagination or memory and putting it into the actual world so you can share it and show it to everyone, most give up after just a few tries.

I'm here to let you know how to make the basics, and the main structure of your drawings, how to make every line and angle work, and everything else that follows will flow smoothly and accordingly just how you want it to be.

Hey, if it doesn't exactly look like in your head, don't beat yourself up. Every developed skill needs practice. So be patient, practice, but most of all,

HAVE FUN!

WHAT IS A FOREST?

A land with a large group of trees that cover more than 10% of that land.

HOW MANY TREES DO FORESTS HAVE?

30% of our planet is covered in Forests which translates to 3 trillion trees.

ARE THERE DIFFERENT TYPES OF FORESTS?

There are 3 major different types: Tropical, Temperate, and Boreal Forests.

WHAT TYPES OF ANIMALS LIVE IN THE FOREST?

Small mammals like rabbits, large mammals like deer, insects like bugs, reptiles like snakes, amphibians like frogs and birds like eagles.

WHAT IS THE SMALLEST FOREST ANIMAL?

A tiny bitty Mouse!

WHAT IS THE BIGGEST FOREST ANIMAL?

The American Black Bear.

WHAT IS THE FASTEST FOREST ANIMAL?

The Hare, running up to 35 miles per hour.

WHAT IS THE TOP PREDATOR YOU CAN FIND IN THE FOREST?

The Eagle! It's at the very top because it doesn't have anyone to fear. It is at the top of the chain without predators.

WHAT ANIMAL IS "COUSIN" TO THE SAVANNA GIRAFFE?

The Okapi, is the closest relative of the giraffe even though they don't live at the same place.

WHAT ARE A BOY DEER AND A GIRL DEER CALLED?

Male deer are called bucks. Females are called does.

WHY ARE HEDGEHOGS CALLED "HEDGEHOGS"?

The "Hedge" part comes from where they build their nests hedges and the "Hog" part comes from the small grunting sound they make.

WHAT IS SOMETHING KANGAROOS CAN'T DO?

Kangaroos can run on 2 legs, walk on 4, jump really high as well as good swimmers but they can't walk backwards!

WHAT BABY KANGAROOS ARE CALLED?

Their babies are called "Joeys".

WHAT ANIMAL IS OUR CLOSEST RELATIVE?

The orangutan! In fact we share close to 97% of DNA.

WHAT DOES "ORANGUTAN" MEAN?

It comes from the Malay words "orang hutan" that means "human of the forest"

HOW MUCH DOES A PANDA EAT IN A SINGLE DAY?

Giant pandas eat as much as 10 kg (22 lb) of bamboo a day.

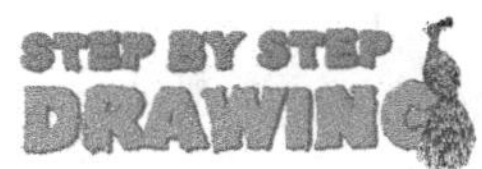

WHAT IS ANOTHER WAY TO CALL A PANTHER?

The "ghost of the forest" for its dark coat helps it hide and stalk prey very easily, especially at night.

WHY DOES A PEACOCK DISPLAY ITS FEATHERS?

They use their feathers for 2 things; 1. to attract future mates and 2. to appear bigger and scare predators.

WHAT ARE BABY RABBITS CALLED?

A young rabbit is called a kit (or kitten).

DO EDIBLE PLANTS GROW IN FORESTS?

Many edible plants, berries and mushrooms grow there, don't eat them though unless a well informed grownup says it's okay. Many plants are poisonous.

BADGER

Badgers are small black and white mammals that are nocturnal. They have thick bodies and short legs that allow them to dig tunnels where they sleep. They grow up to be around 3 feet long and weight around 22 pounds. They are carnivorous and are known to be the most fearless mammal in the world.

BEAR

Bears are mammals that eat meat grasses, herbs and fruit and fish. They have a shaggy thick coat of fur that keeps them really warm during winter time when they hibernate. Even though they are large they can run to 25 mph and with their claws climb up trees and hills. They have big ears but their sense of smell is excellent.

BUG

Badgers are small black and white mammals that are nocturnal. They have thick bodies and short bodies that allow them to dig tunnels where they sleep. They grow up to be a meter long and weight around 22 pounds They are carnivorous and are known to be the most fearless mammal in the world.

COYOTE

Coyotes are related to dogs and look a lot a like but with pointed ears and drooped long tail. They are nocturnal predators, carnivores and capable of running at speeds up to 65 km/hr and they can jump horizontal distances of up to 4 meters. They are born blind until they open their eyes ten days after and they can live up to 10 years in the wild.

CRICKET

Crickets are nocturnal insects that means they are cold blooded. They chirp to attract a mate, but only male crickets do the chirping noise by rubbing their wings together. The chirping varies depending the temperature, the higher the temperature the higher the rate. They are considered a sign of good luck in many cultures.

DEER

The deer are part of the cervidae family, meaning they have a lot of relatives like moose, reindeer, elk and more. A boy deer is called a "buck" and a girl is called "stag" an a group of them are called a "herd". They are born with white spots on their back and when they grow older they lose them as well they stay with their mother until they turned one.

DRAGONFLY

Dragonflies are flying insects that vary of color their bodies are long and their wings transparent. They great hunters and carnivores, meaning they eat other smaller insects like mosquitoes. They can eat 100 mosquitoes a day making them one of the best insects hunters. They can fly in every direction and hoover like helicopters.

EAGLE

Eagles are one of the most powerful birds, making them a predator without having anyone above them on the chain. They have excellent eyesight and strong talons which help them catch their prey. There are 60 different types of eagle and
they lay their eggs up in high hills or in tall trees.

FOX

Foxes are small agile runners that live in family groups. They are carnivore but they also eat berries and fruit. They have a large fluffy tail that has various purposes. It helps them stay warm in the winter, store food on wintertime and for balance while running.
A female fox is called a vixen, and the male is called a dog.

HARE

Hares are usually confused with rabbits but they have some differences. Hares are larger than rabbits with longer ears and their babies are born with their eyes open.
They are great jumpers and can run up to 72 kph (45 mph).

HEDGEHOG

Hedgehogs are small little creatures that sleep in the day and come out at night. They really like their sleep so sometimes they choose to hibernate which means they hole themselves up and stay in a sleeping state for winter. They don't usually use their eyes to hunt, they rely more on their smell and hearing sense. Hedgehog have around 5000 spikes they can raise and lower in command if they feel threatened or safe.

JACKAL

Jackals are related to coyotes and wolfs. They are nocturnal hunters, usually doing it alone but sometimes join small packs for better results. Jackals choose a partner for their whole life.

KANGAROO

Kangaroos are designed for jumping with two powerful back legs and strong long tail that helps them to jump around and keep their balance. They can grow to be between five and six feet and weight around 50 to 120 pounds. Kangaroos have babies called "Joeys" and they carry them on their belly pouch for eight months unti they are ready to stand and jump on their own.

KOALA

Koalas are often called small bears but they are marsupials that eat eucalyptus leaves and nothing more. They have sharp claws that help them climb trees in which they sleep all day long. Usually between 18 and 22 hours.

LYNX

Lynx are small savage cats that have short tails and large paws that help them walk through the snow. They usually weight around 11 pounds and are size of a domestic cat.
Their fur is a yellow-brown with a little grey and their ears are black. They are lonely animals not only when they hunt but in their everyday activities.

OKAPI

Okapis are herbivore animals that grow to be almost six feet tall. They are white and black stripped. People usually think they are related to zebras but they are not, they are related to giraffe. The strippes they have help them camoflage and escape predators.

ORANGUTAN

Orangutan are from the apes family and they are covered with reddish fur. They grow to be five feet and weigh up to 100 more that 200 pounds. Their arms are extremely long some males can stretch their arms 2m from fingertip to fingertip. They live long lives up to 30 or 40 years. They spend most of their time up in the trees swinging the day away.

PANDA

Pandas have black and white fur, always two black patches around their eyes. Even though Pandas are born just a few cm long and about 100 grams, they grow up to be more than 300 pounds. Pandas only eat bamboo and they eat 10 kg a day!

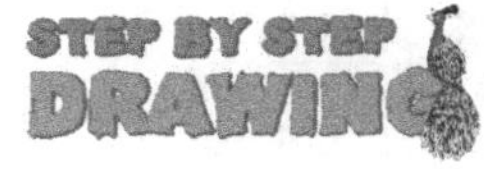

PANTHER

Panthers are a black jaguar, they usually have spots but their fur is so dark they are almost invisible. They are great swimmers as well as very strong climbers. Panthers have good hearing, extremely good eyesight which makes them really good hunters.

PEACOCK

Peacocks are known for their colorful and beautiful feathers. Male peacocks also known as "Peafowl" use their feathers to dance and attract a mate and also to appear bigger and scare predators away. Their feathers fan around them and stretch almost 2 meters in length.

PRAYING MANTIS

Praying Mantis is an insect that gets its name because of the way their 2 front legs are positioned, it reminded people of a praying position. They are carnivores, eating other smaller insects that's why many gardeners like them because they help get rid of insects that eat their beautiful plants or crops.

RABBIT

Wild Rabbits are very sociable, they live in groups.
They dig up tunnels underground called warrens where they
sleep. They are born with their eyes closed and no fur.
Rabbit's ears are long and they grow to 10 cm!
Their eyes at the sides of their head which means they can see
all around them making them super alert and cautious.

RACCOON

Raccoons are a nocturnal mammal that are known for their balck
masks. During the winter they sleep for longer periods of time but they
do not hibernate. They are excellent swimmers and great hunters
because they are very sneaky. Racoons have a very varied diet of fruits,
seeds, nuts, birds' eggs and plants.

RAMPHICELUS

Ramphocelus is a colorful bird. Male Ramphocelus may be black with
yellow, red or orange and female Ramphocelus is usually brown or
greyish combined with a dull yellow, red or orange.

SNAKE

Snakes are reptiles and they don't have eyelids, ears, arms or legs. They have long and slender bodies and their skin is covered in scales. Their eyesight is okay but they can taste scents with their tongue when they flick them in and out. Snakes don't have a voice but they can hiss. Because they are cold blooded they like warm weather.

SQUIRREL

Squirrels are furry rodents with big eyes and fluffy tails. Squirrels are agile runners and skillful climbers and can glide from tree to tree. Squirrels mostly eat seeds, fruits and nuts. They have really large eyes which helps them stay alert and escape predators.

WILD PIG

Wild Pig can grow very very big, wighting a few hundred pounds and measuring 5 feet long. They have black and brown fur and hooves. Their sight is not all that good but they have a great sense of smell. they love to cover themselves in mud, it helps them cool off and protects their skin of the sun.

Stop right there!

Scan this code to get FREE goodies from the Step by Step Book Series!

littlepencilpress.com

TWO WAYS TO WORK WITH THIS BOOK, CHOOSE THE ONE YOU LIKE THE MOST!

HAVE FUN DRAWING!

Simply draw the darker lines and ignore the geometrical shapes, we show you the Step by Step for every drawing.

OR

IMPROVE YOUR DRAWING TECHNIQUE!

Follow every step, starting with the geometrical shapes in a lighter line and over those, draw with darker lines your final animal. With practice, this technique will help you draw anything you want, simply starting by geometrical lines will help you visualize how the final image will look in your drawing area and the traces you will need to create something amazing!

REMEMBER! IF YOU FIND THIS BOOK TOO EASY OR TOO HARD TO FOLLOW, WE HAVE OTHER STEP BY STEP BOOKS WITH DIFFERENT LEVELS OF DIFFICULTY.

DIFFICULTY LEVELS FROM EASIEST TO HARDEST:

1 Step by Step Drawing Zoo Animals

2 Step by Step Ocean Animals

3 Step by Step Fat pets

4 Step by Step Forest Animals

5 Step by Step Cute Mythical Creatures

EXAMPLE

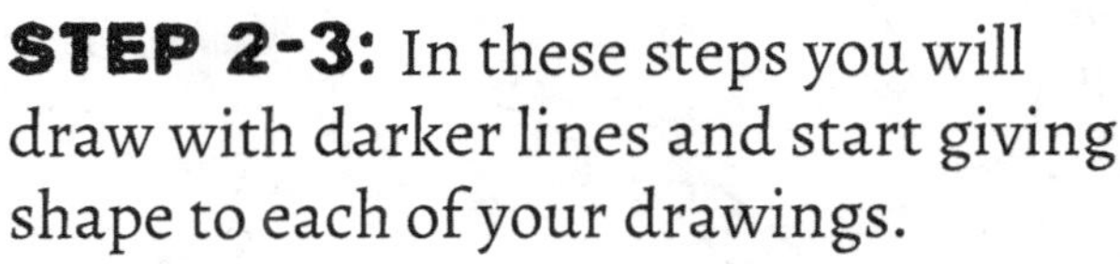

STEP 1: Simplify in geometrical figures the shape of the animal. Remember this will be your guide and over those lines, you will draw your masterpiece so, make them lighter.

STEP 2-3: In these steps you will draw with darker lines and start giving shape to each of your drawings.

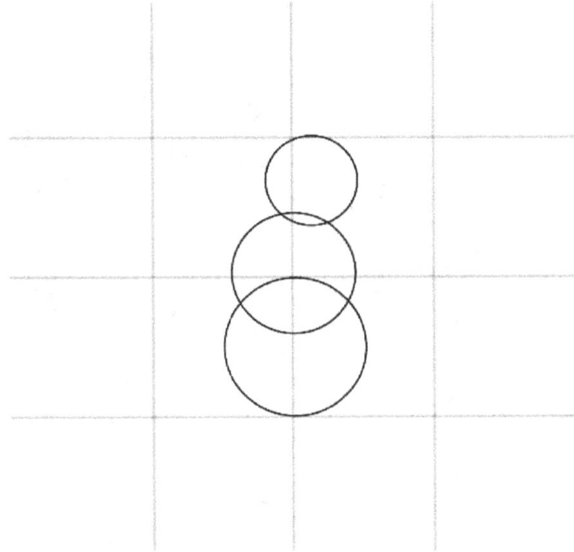

STEP 4: Add details! Now that you have your final shape, we need to add details that will make your drawing look amazing, you can add way more details than the ones we show. Always remember practice makes perfect and you can always redraw what you didn't like but you can never love what you never draw. Be creative!

STEP 5: To finish up your art you just need to erase your geometrical lines and everything else you do not like, add shading if you want and you are done!

BADGER

TRY IT HERE!

BADGER

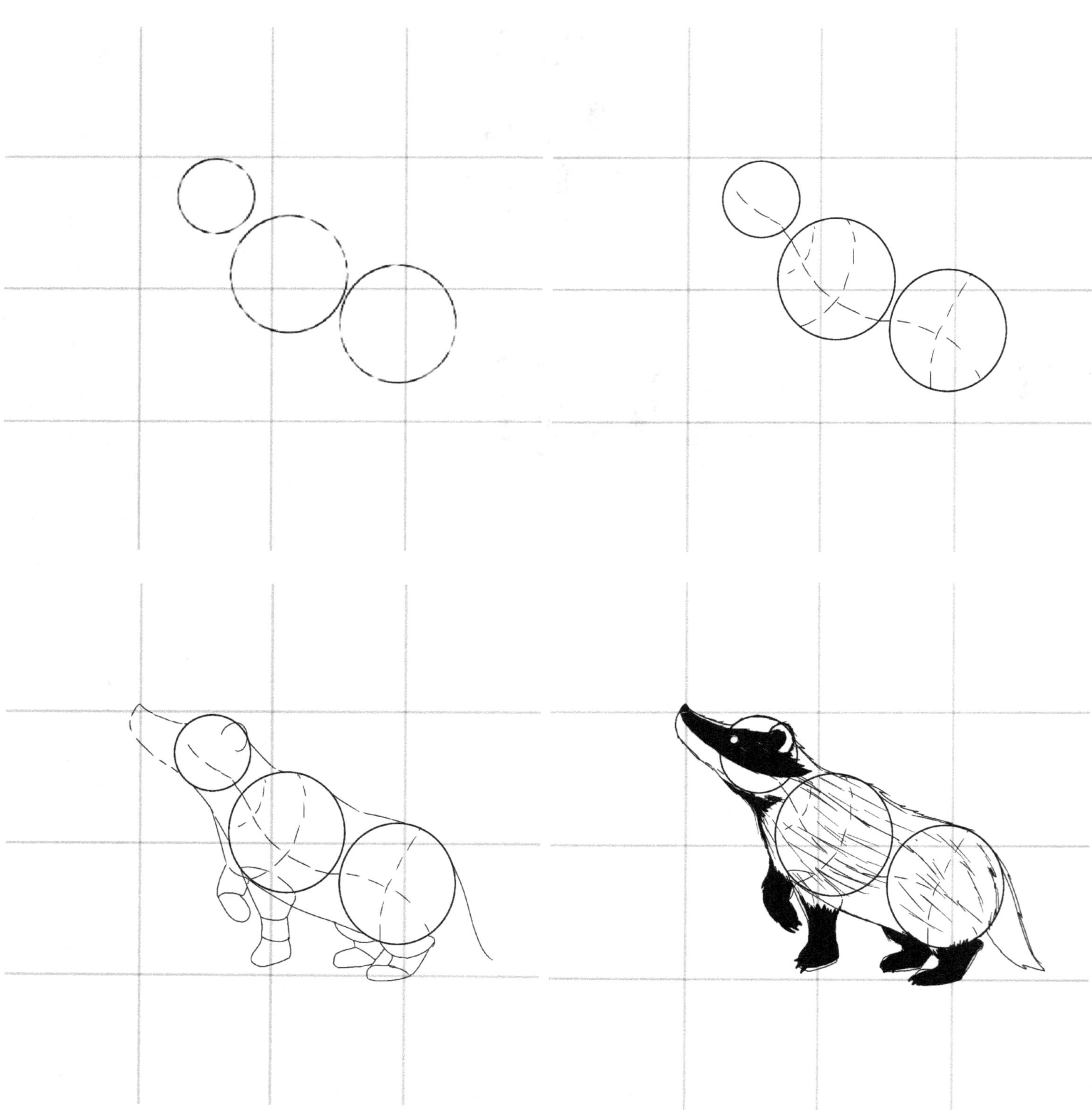

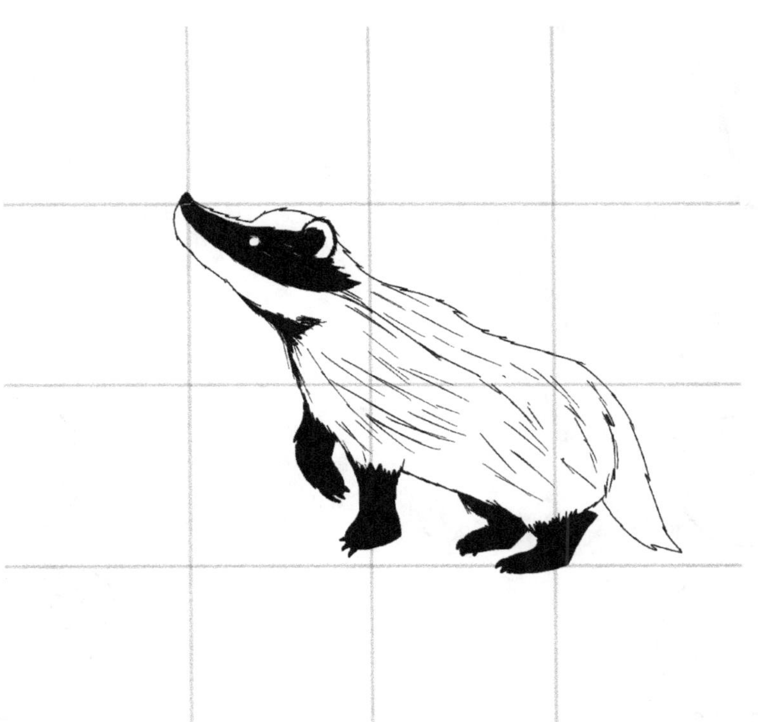

TRY IT HERE!

BEAR

TRY iT HERE!

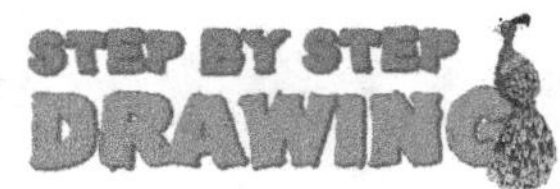

BEAR

TRY IT HERE!

BEAR

TRY it HERE!

BUG

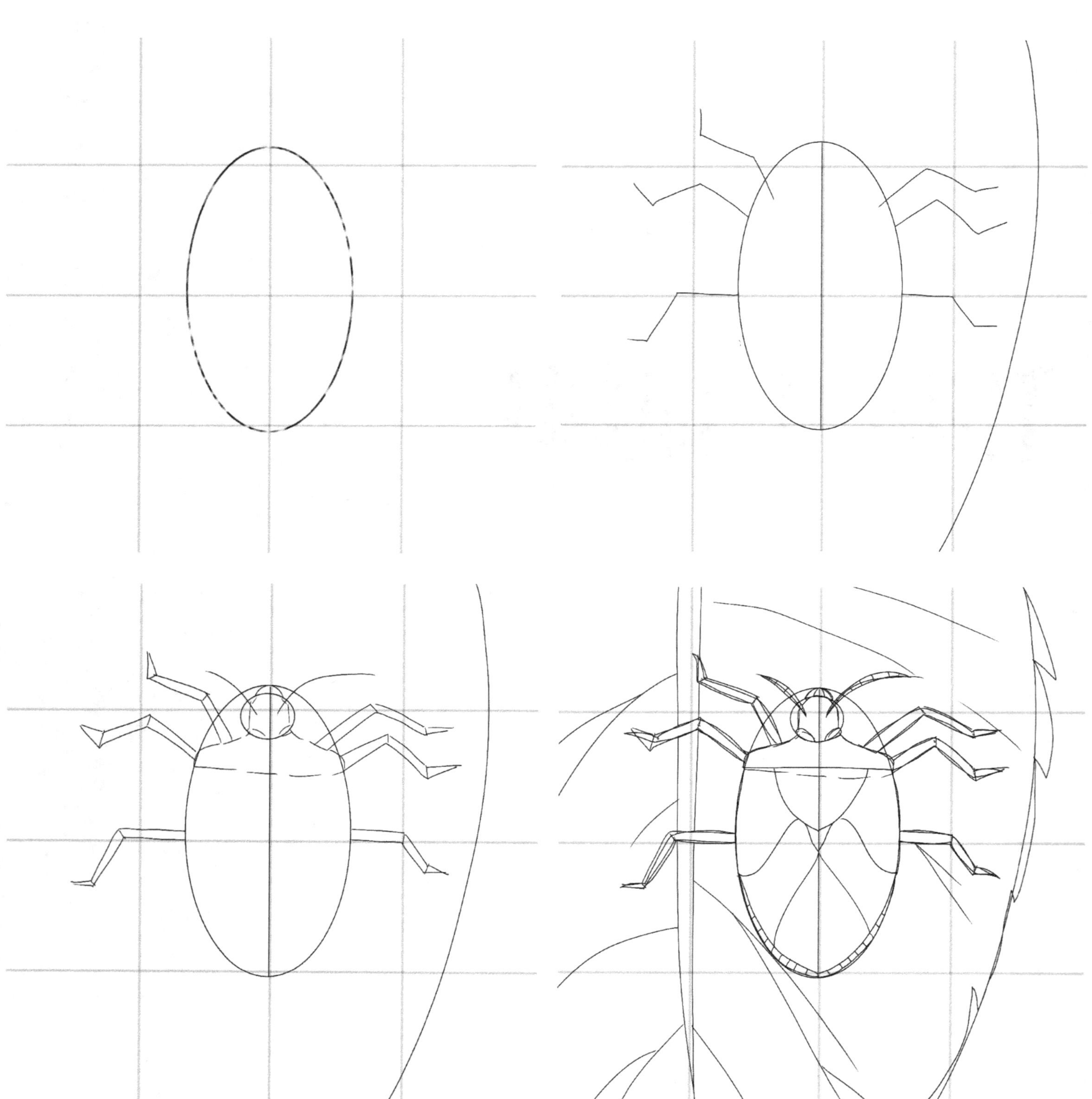

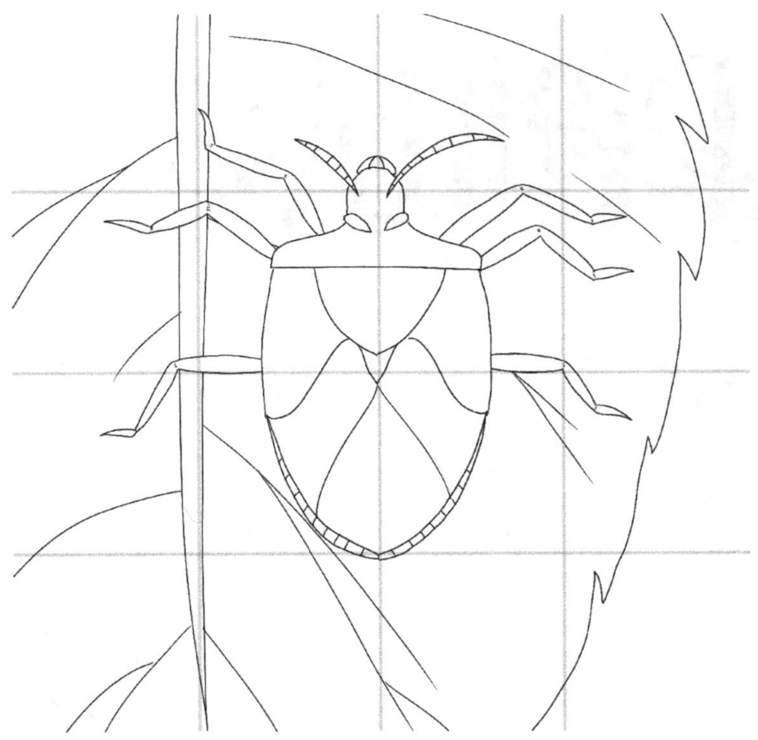

TRY iT HERE!

CATERPILLAR

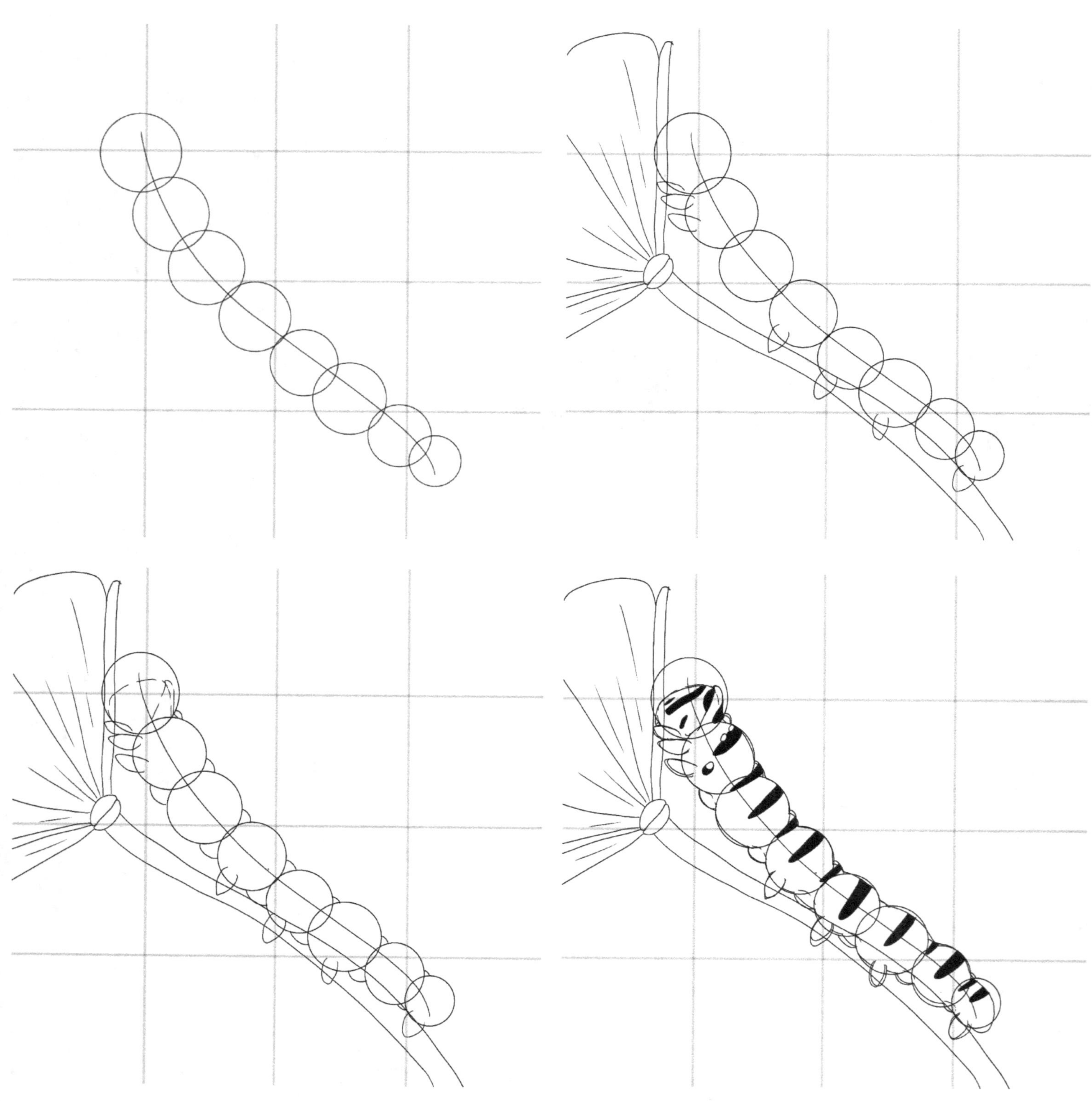

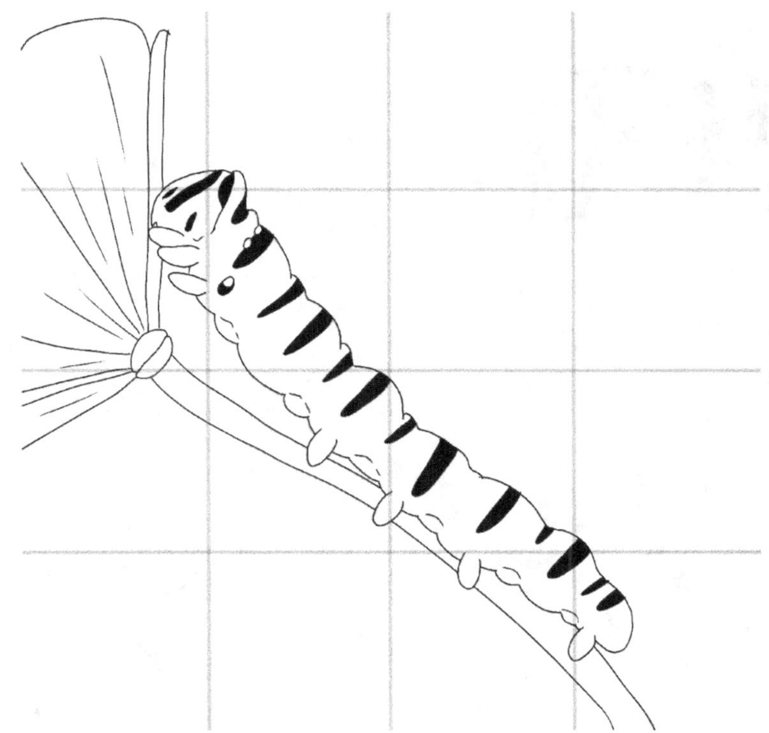

TRY it HERE!

COYOTE

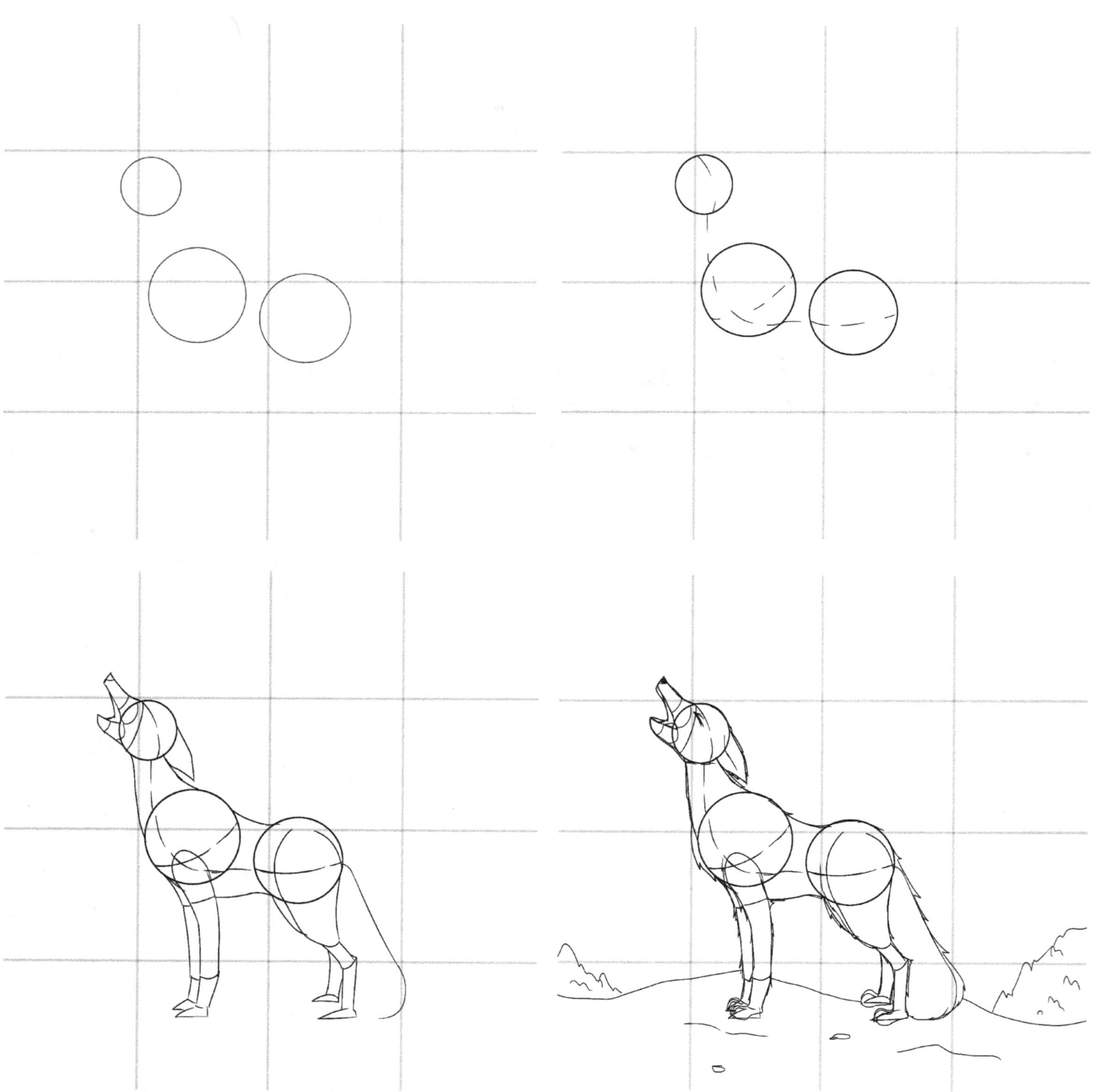

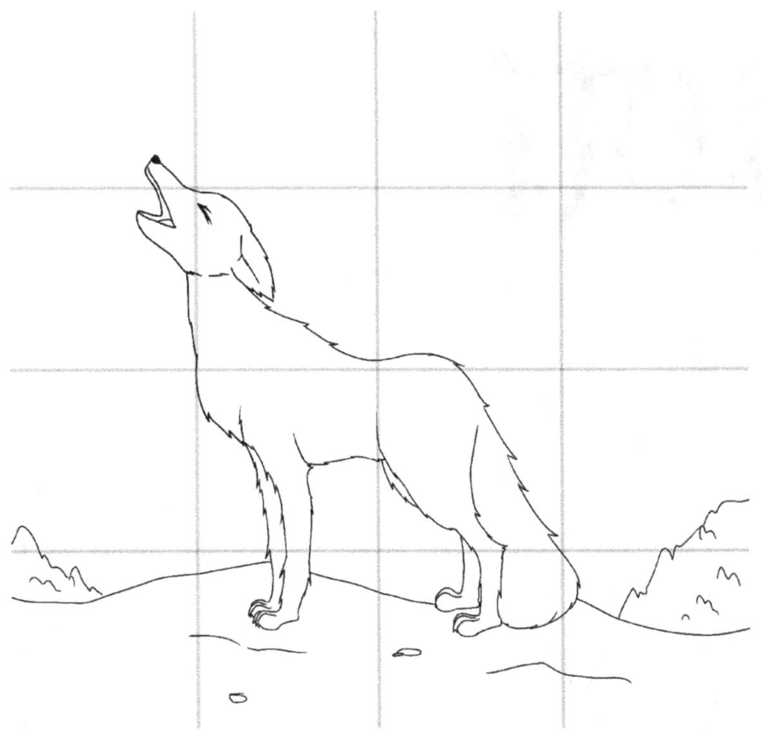

TRY IT HERE!

COYOTE

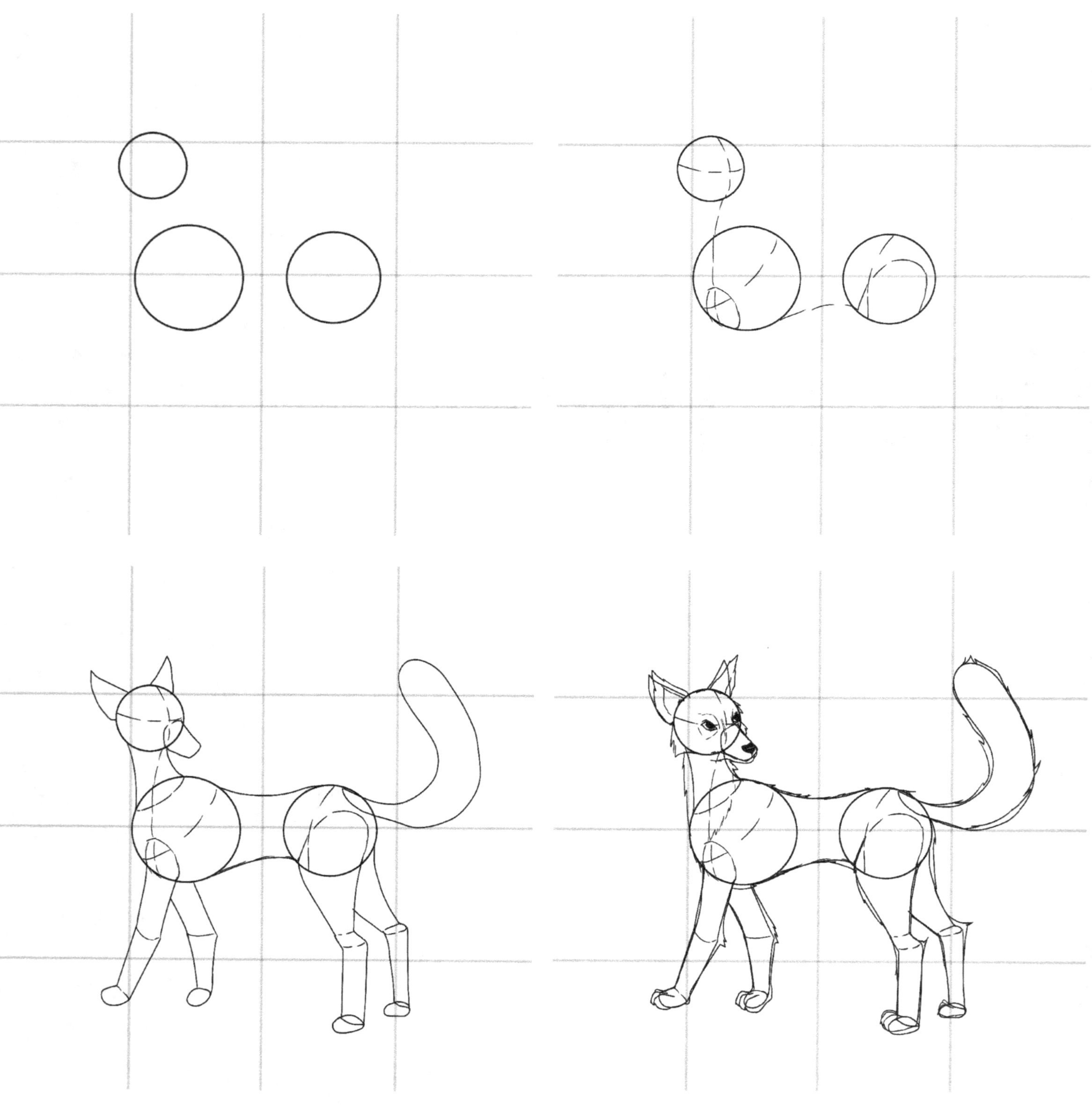

TRY it HERE!

CRICKET

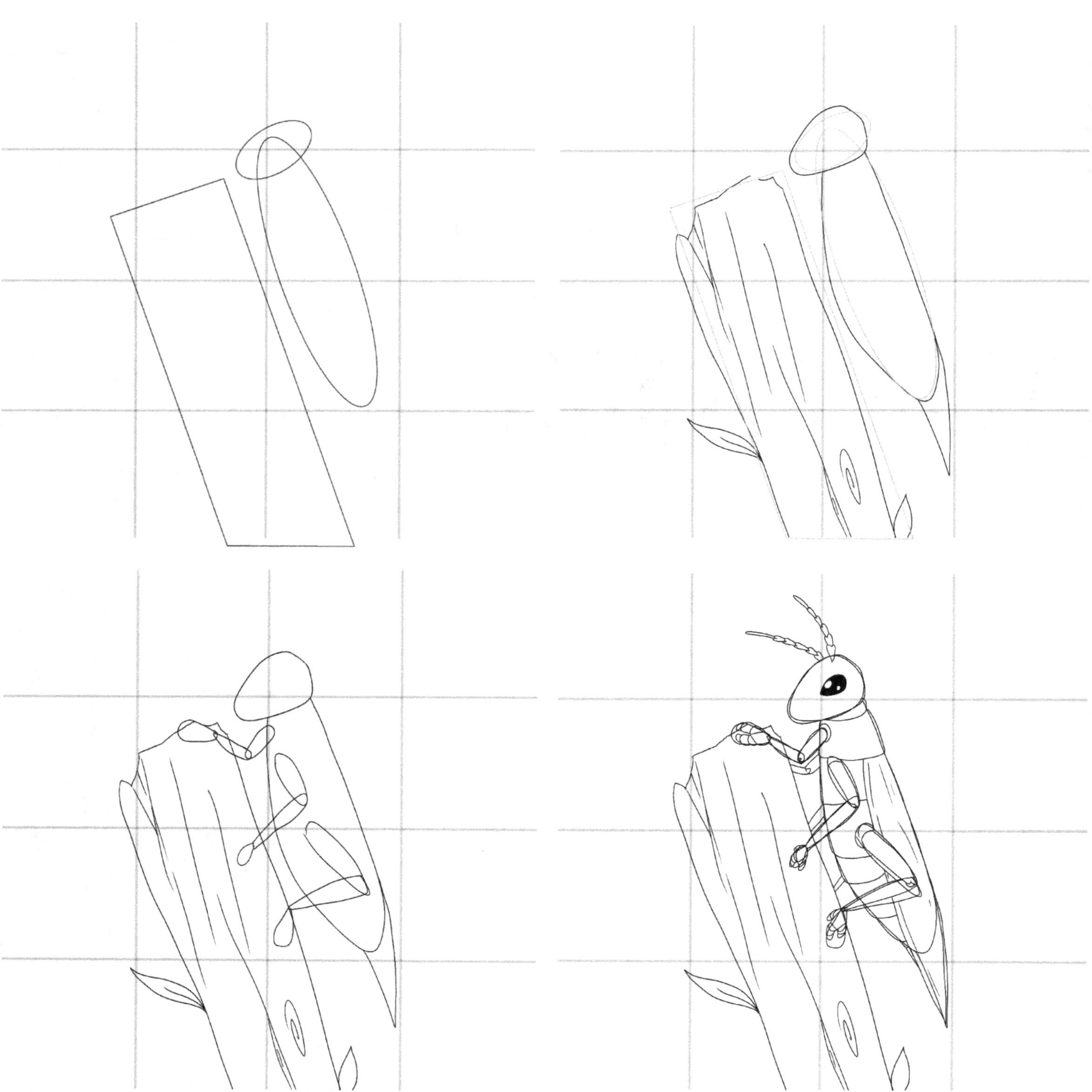

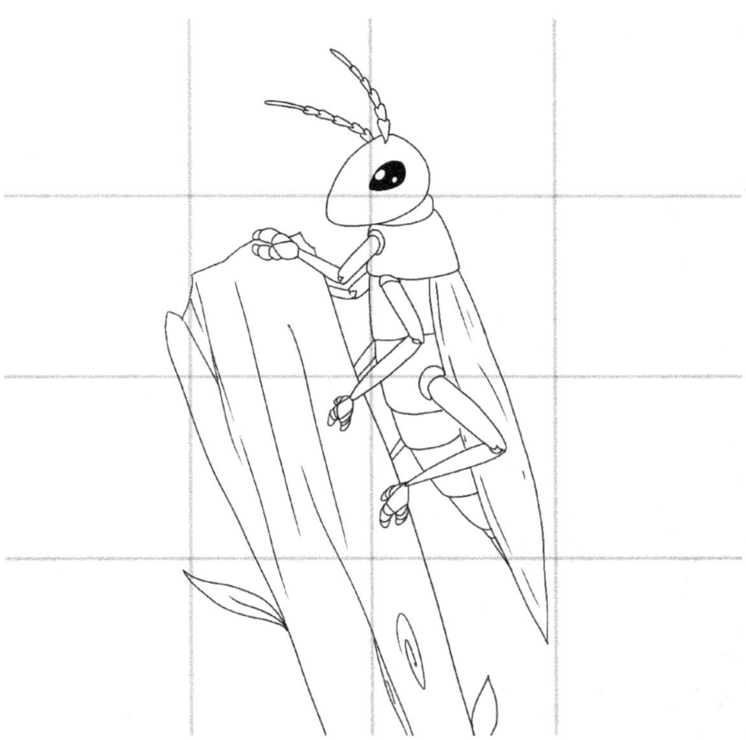

TRY IT HERE!

DEER

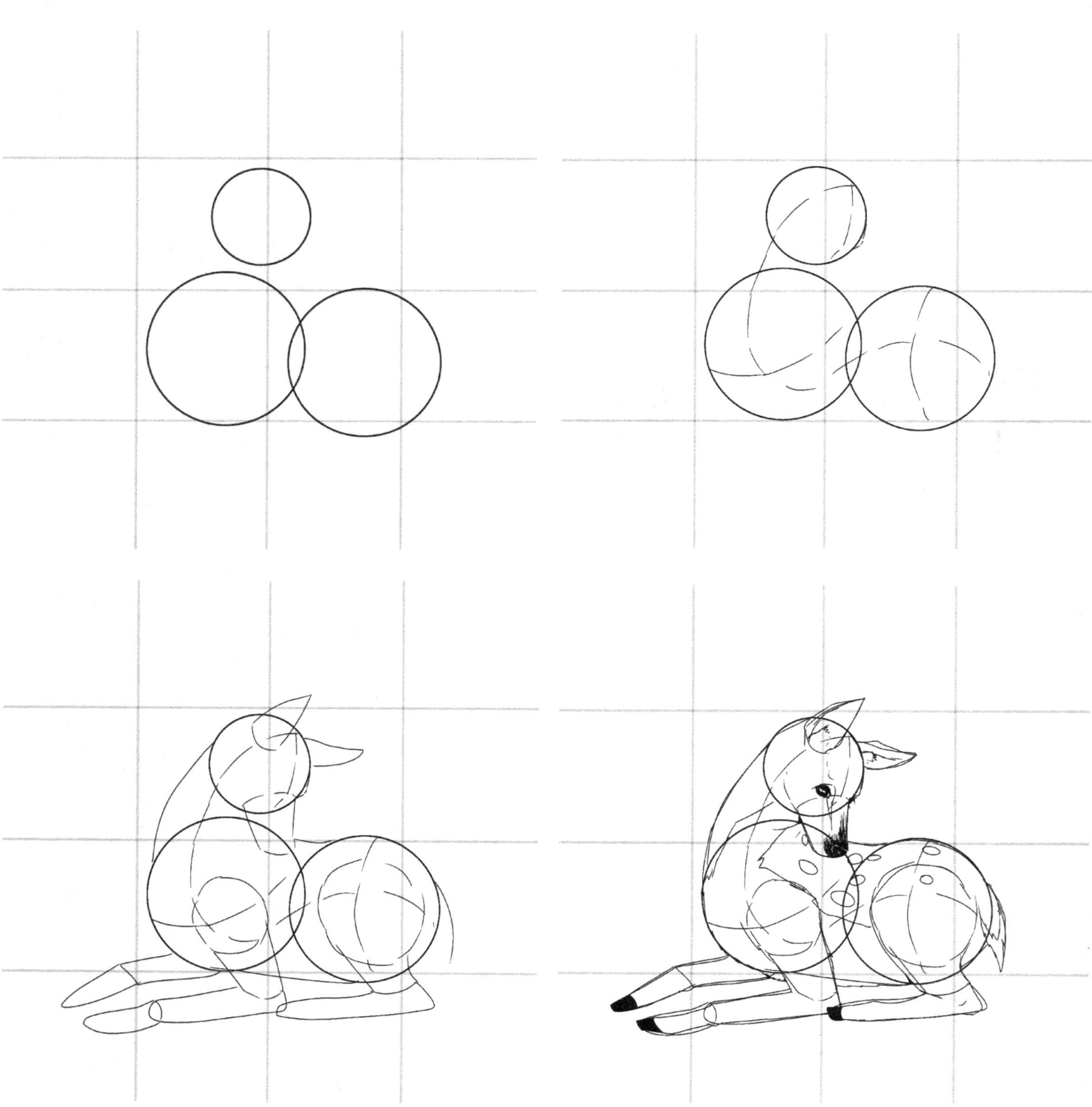

TRY IT HERE!

DEER

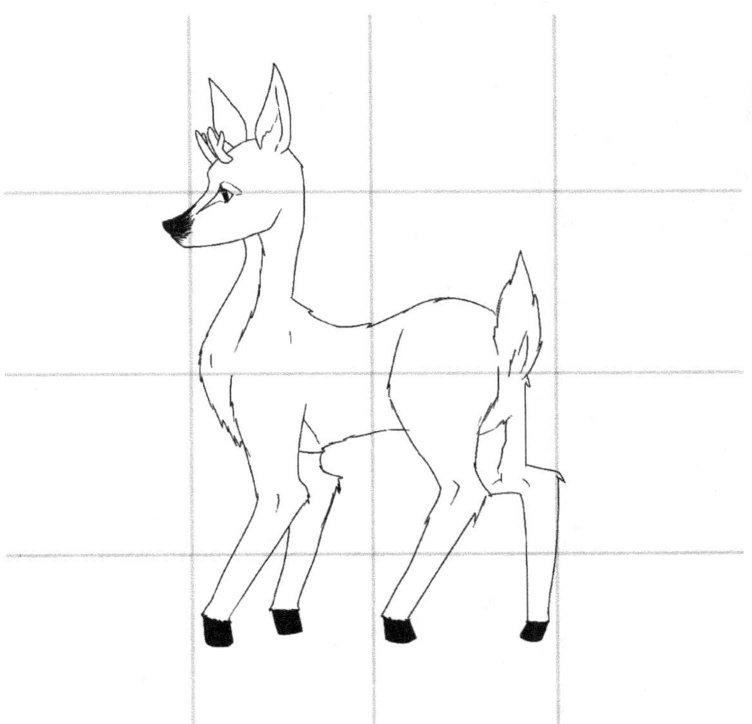

TRY IT HERE!

DEER

TRY it HERE!

DEER

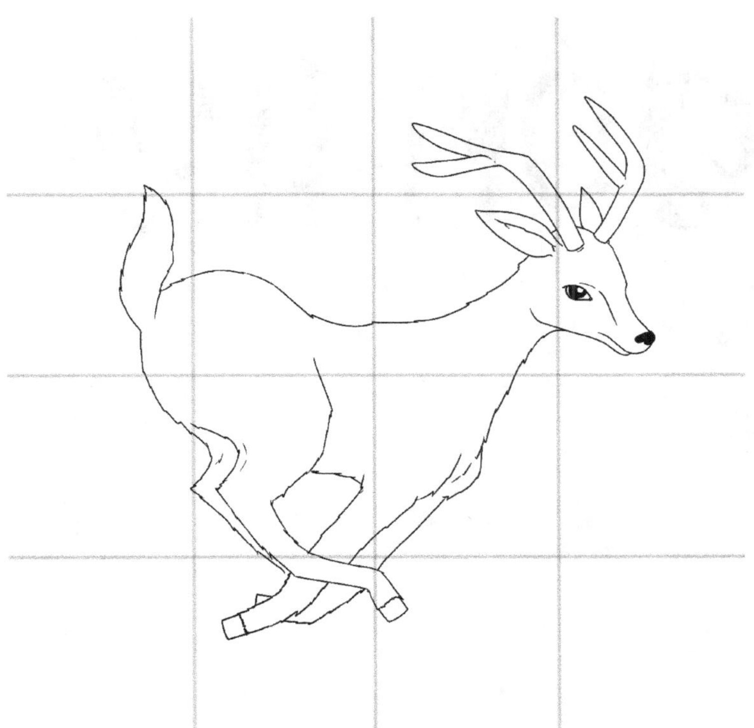

TRY iT HERE!

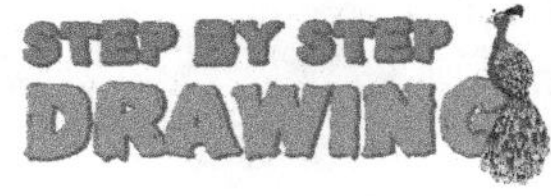

DRAGON-FLY

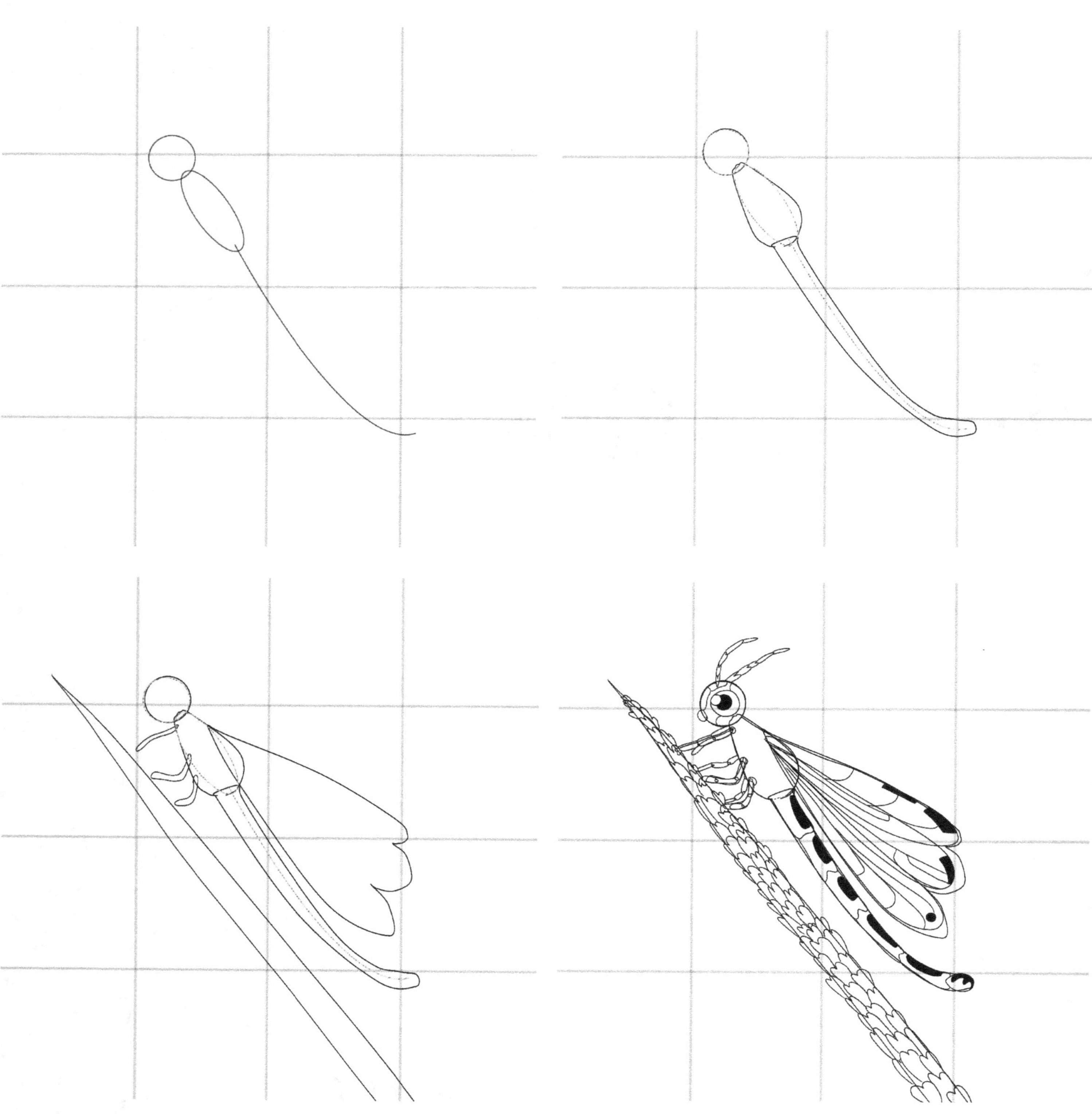

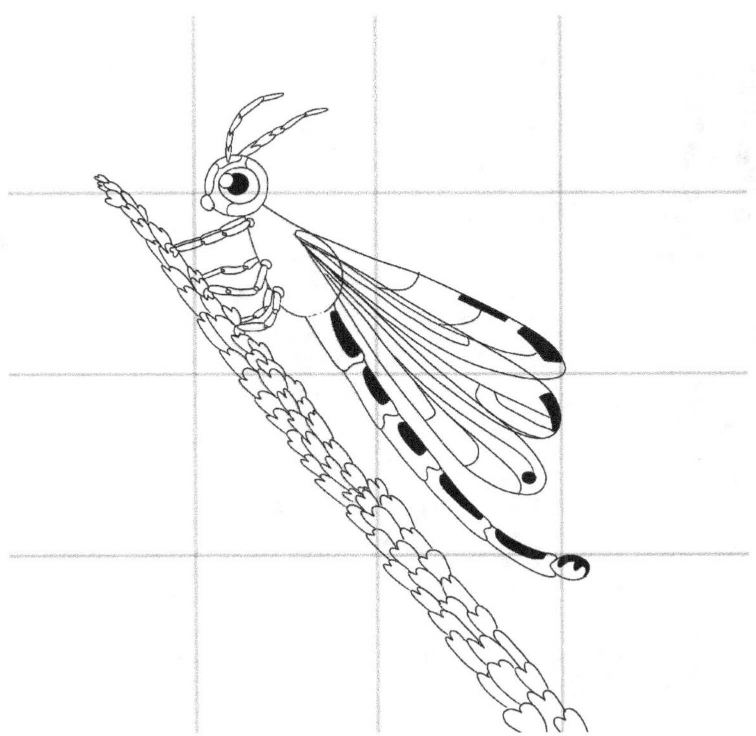

TRY IT HERE!

EAGLE

TRY it HERE!

EAGLE

TRY it HERE!

FOX

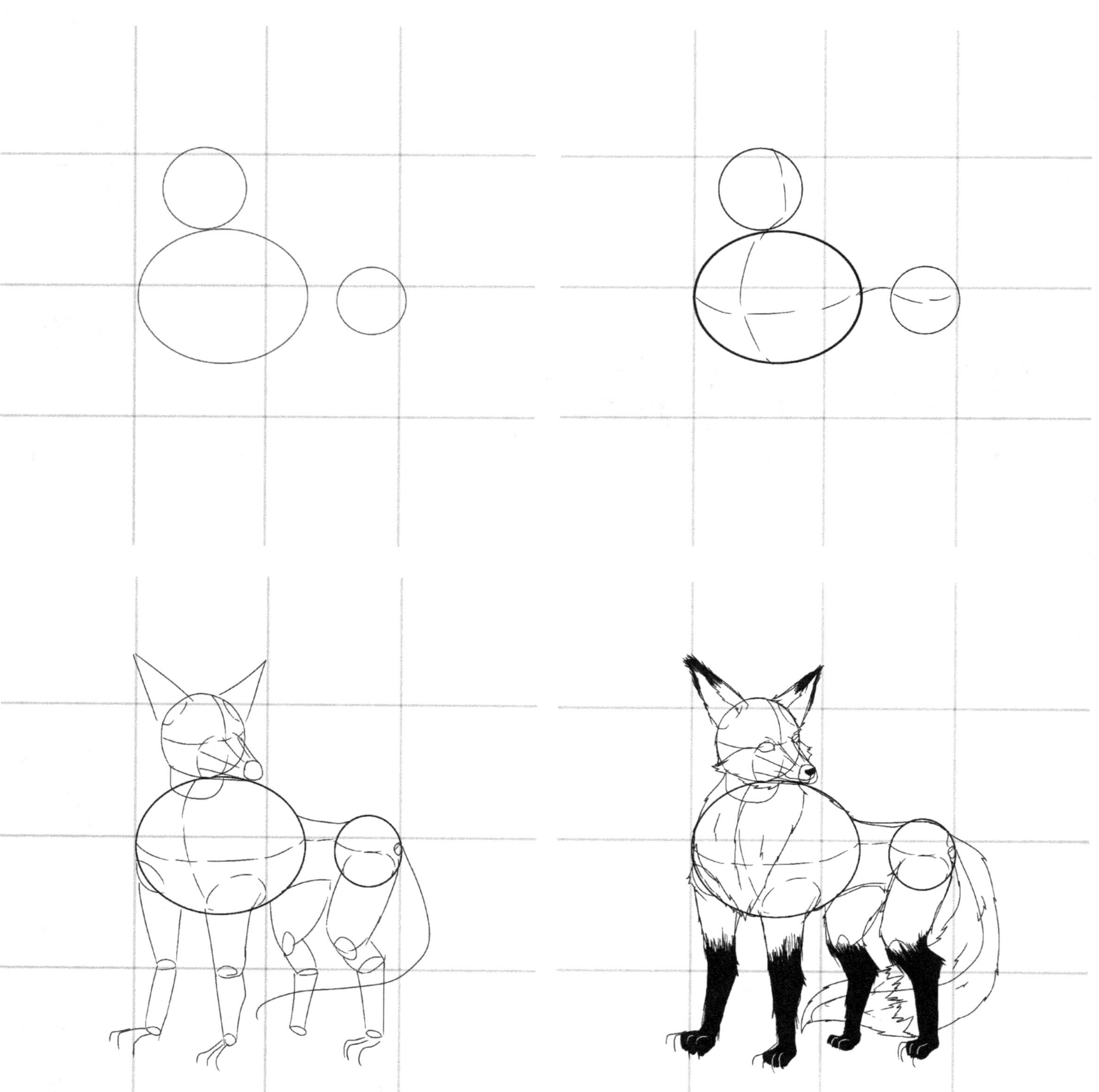

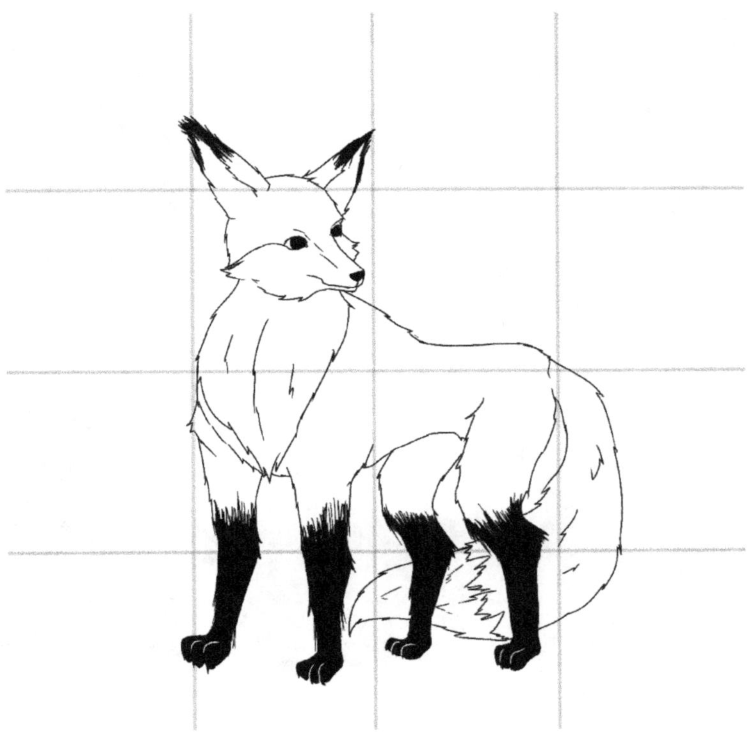

TRY IT HERE!

FOX

TRY it HERE!

HARE

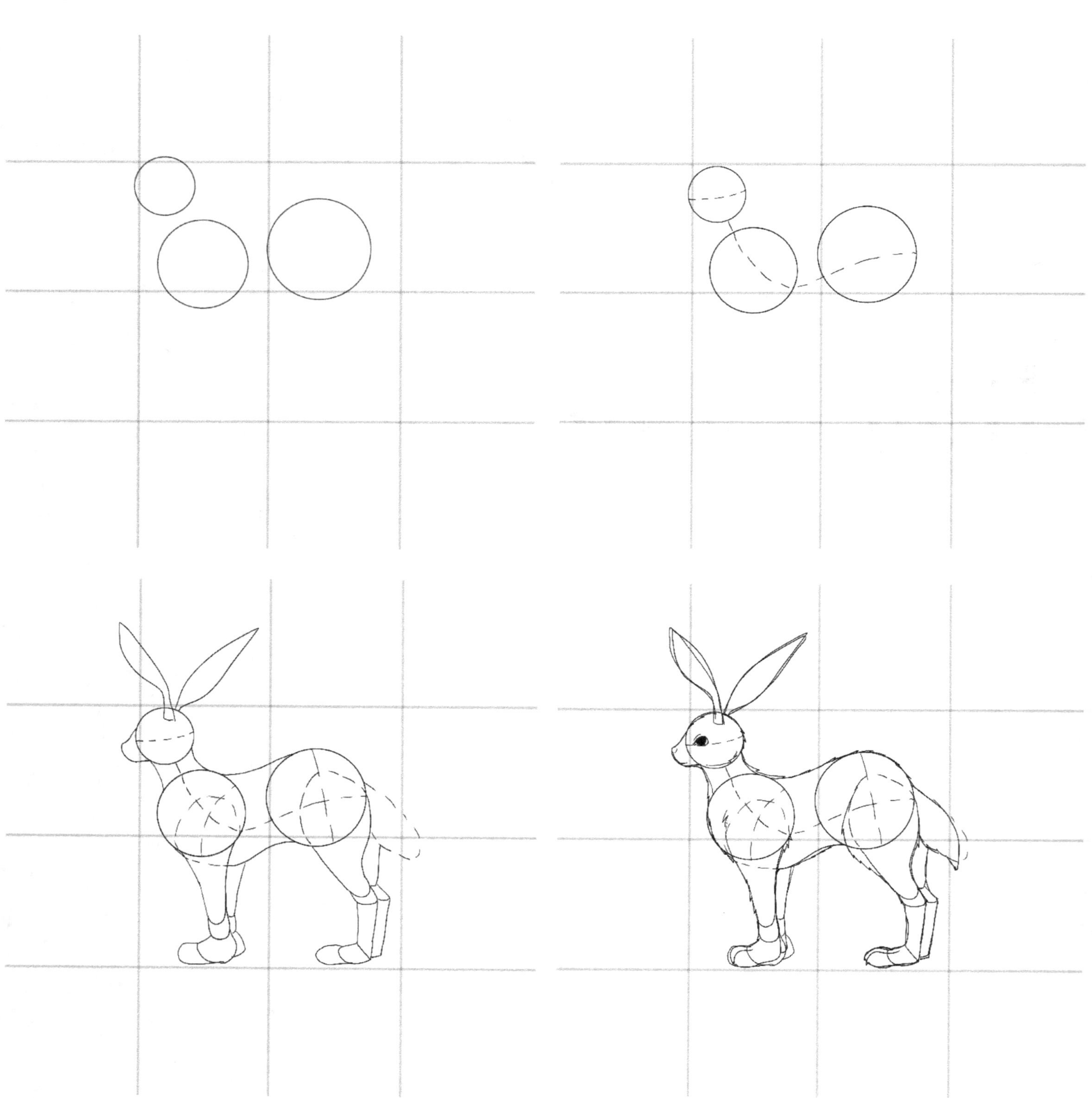

TRY IT HERE!

HARE

TRY it HERE!

HEDGEHOG

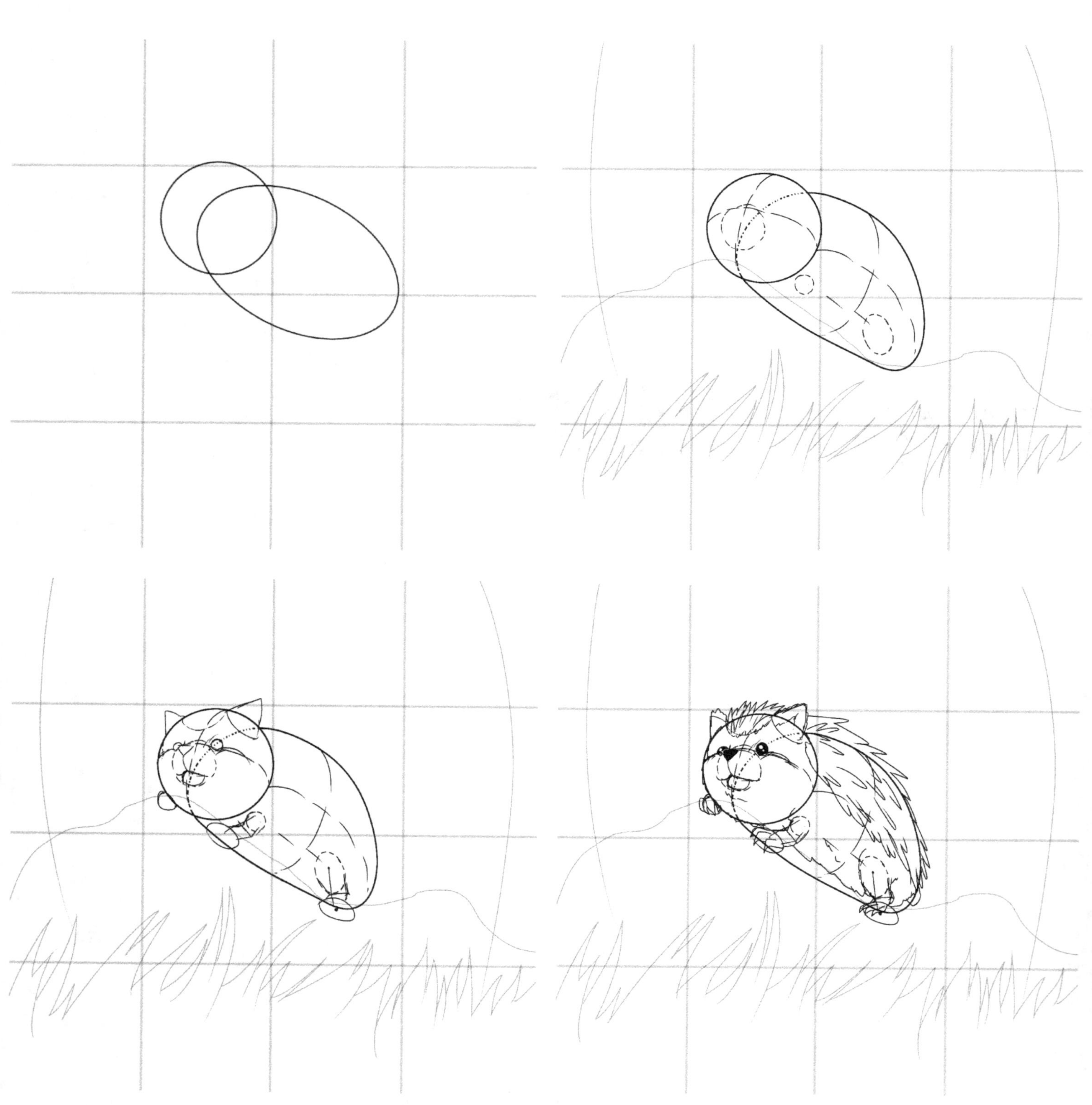

TRY IT HERE!

HEDGEHOG

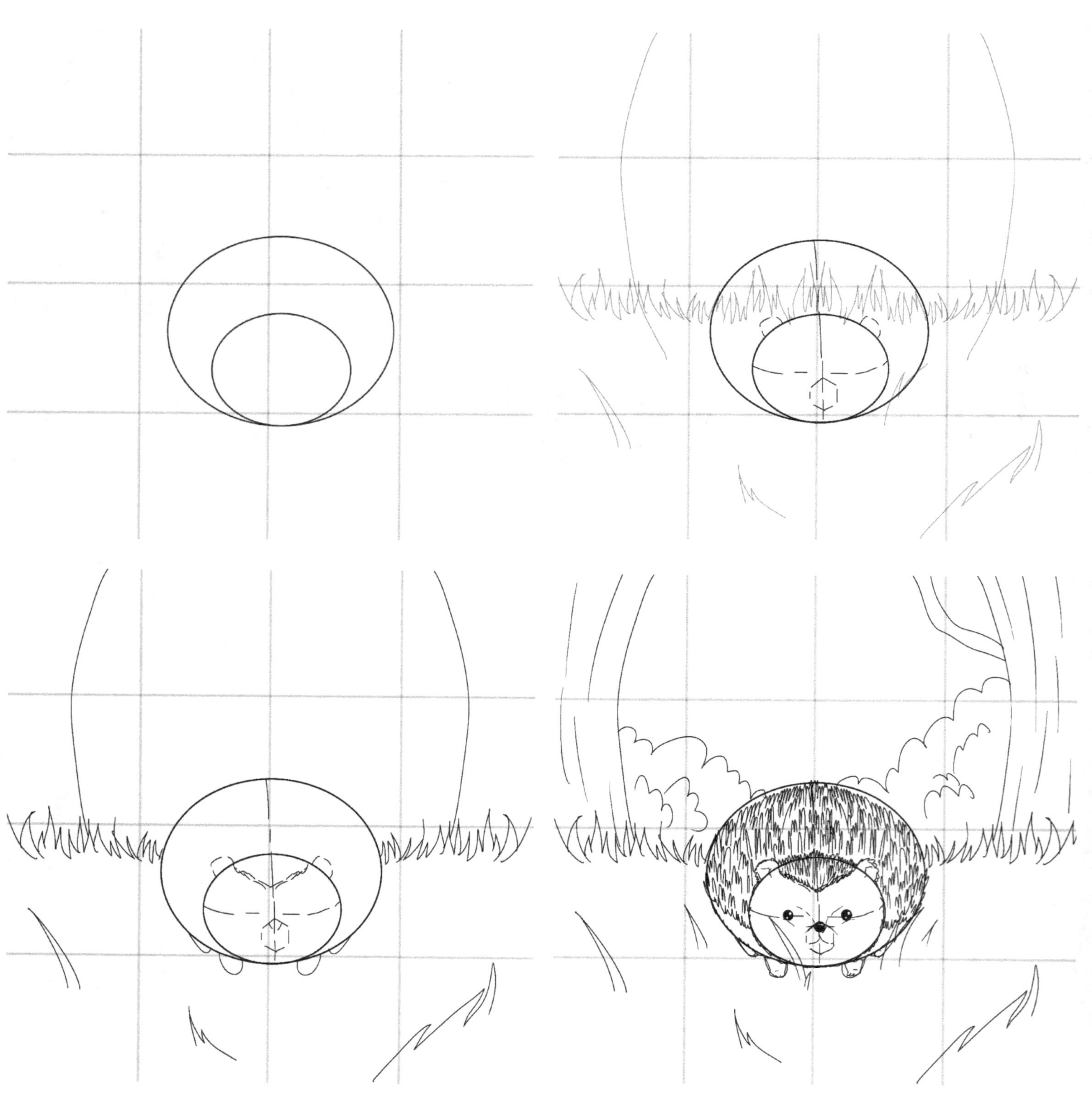

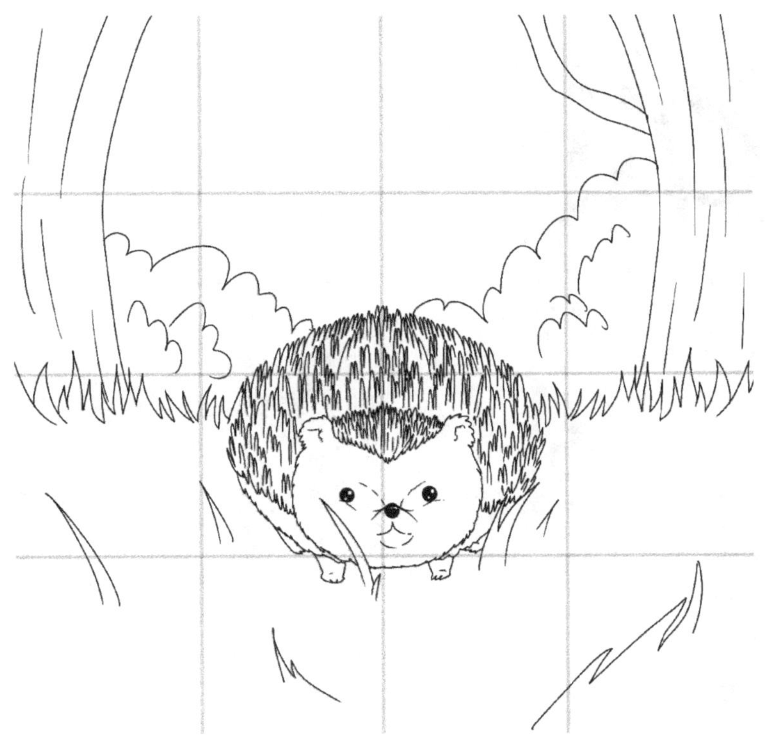

TRY IT HERE!

JACKAL

TRY IT HERE!

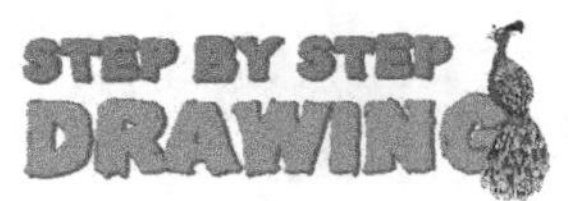

JACKAL

TRY IT HERE!

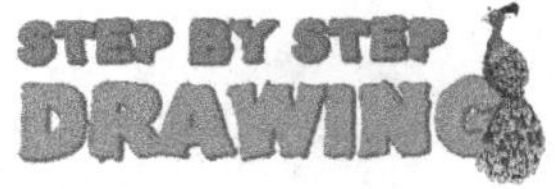

KANGARO

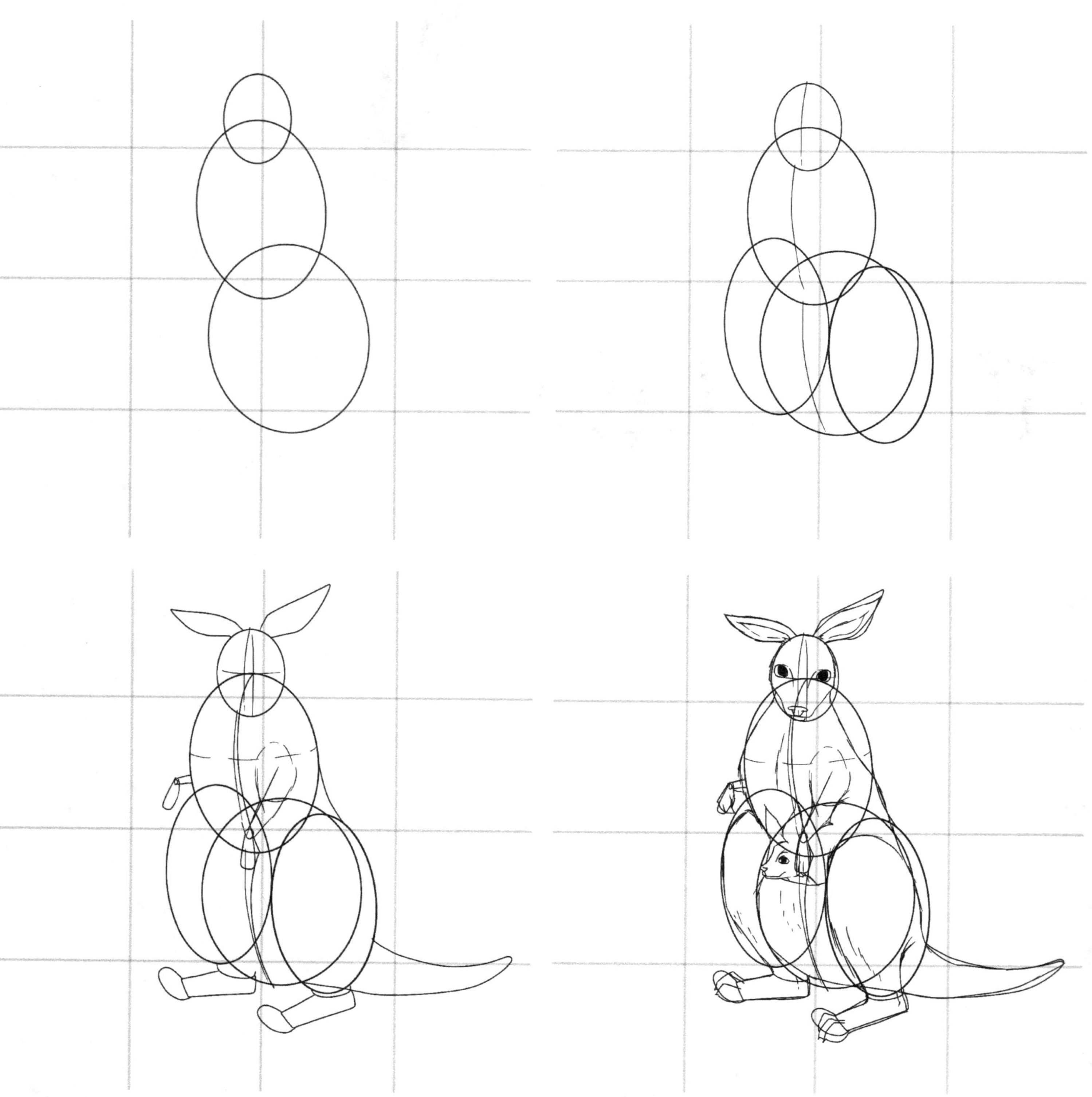

TRY iT HERE!

KOALA

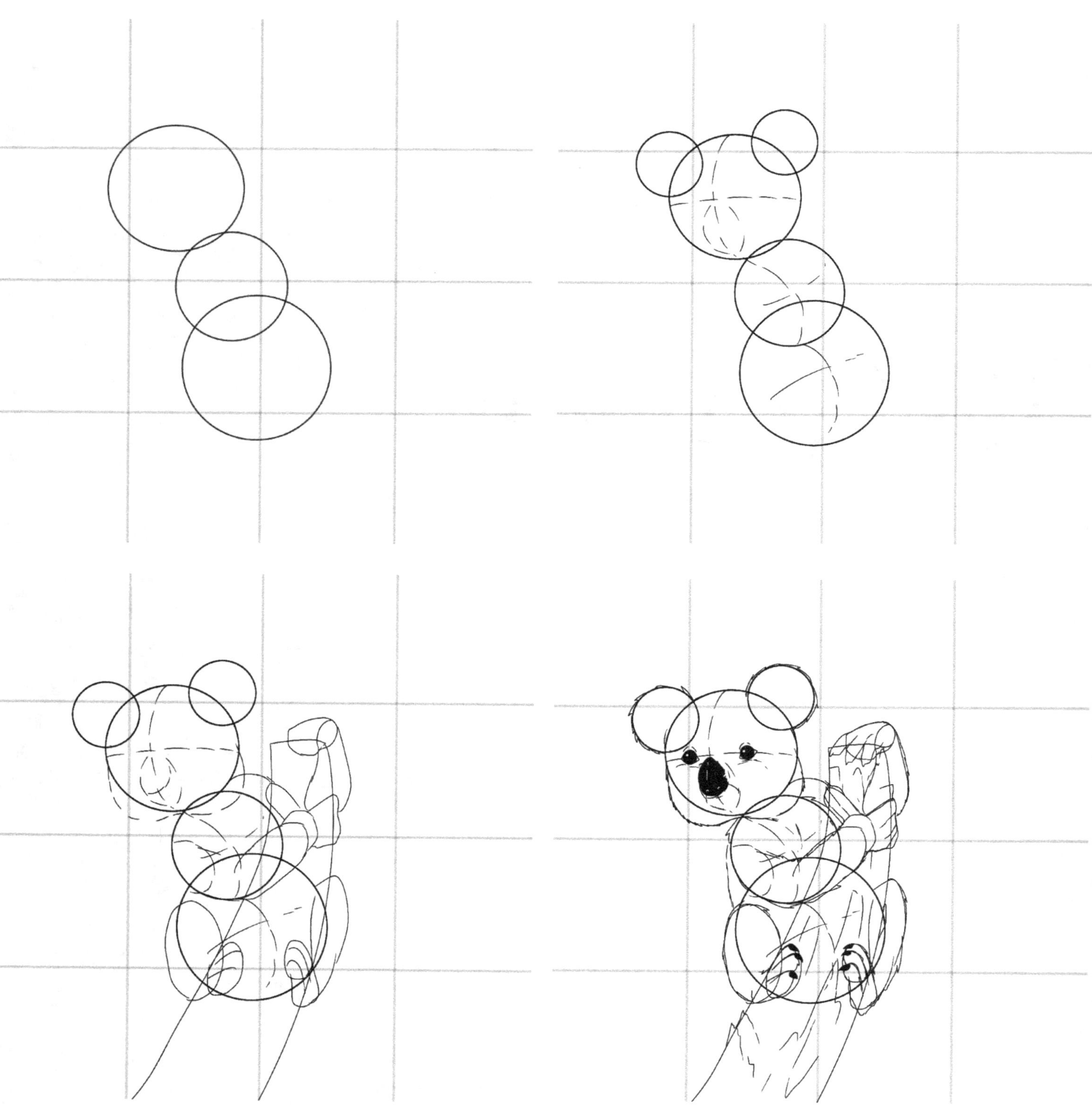

TRY IT HERE!

KOALA

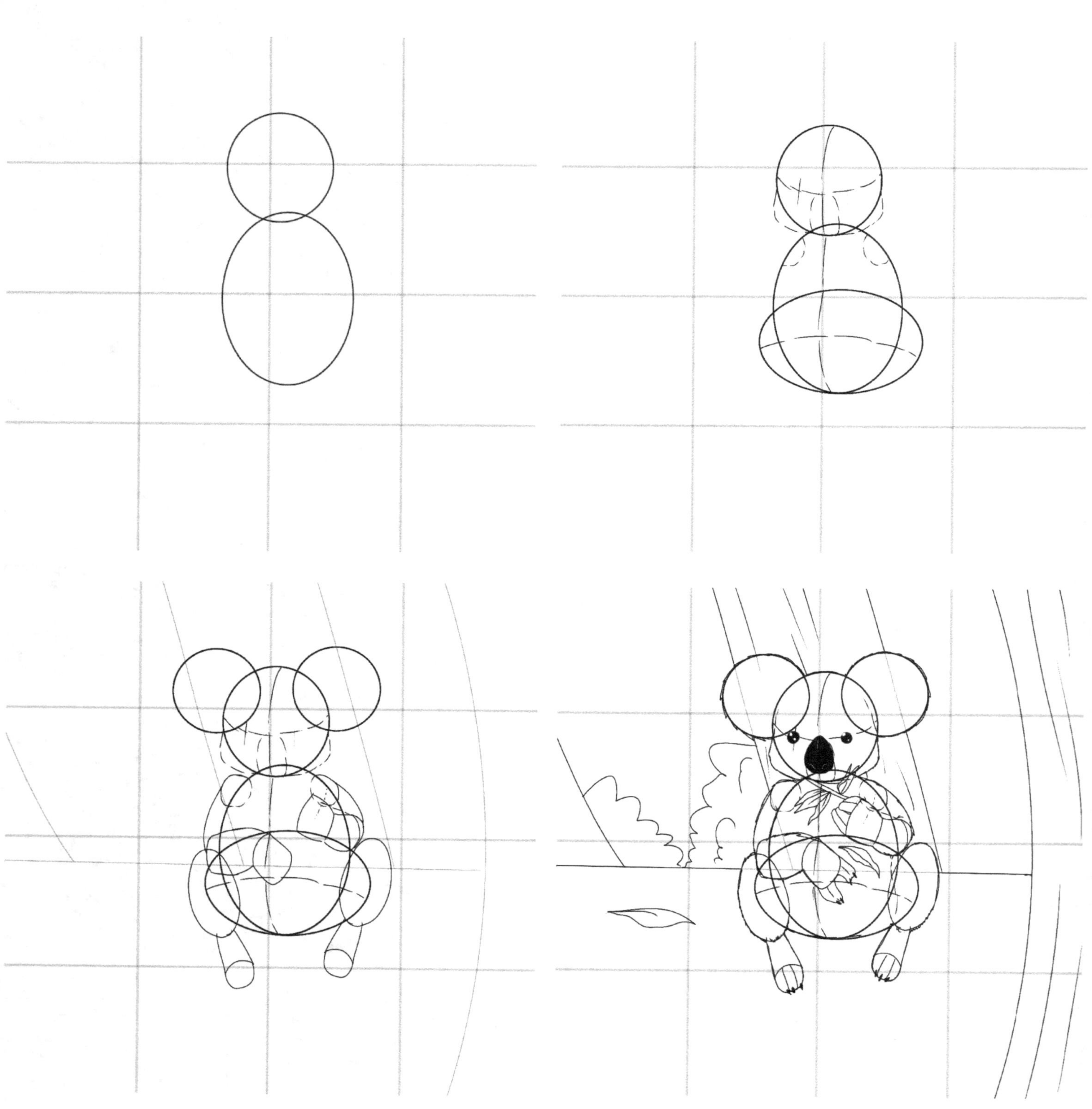

TRY it HERE!

Lynx

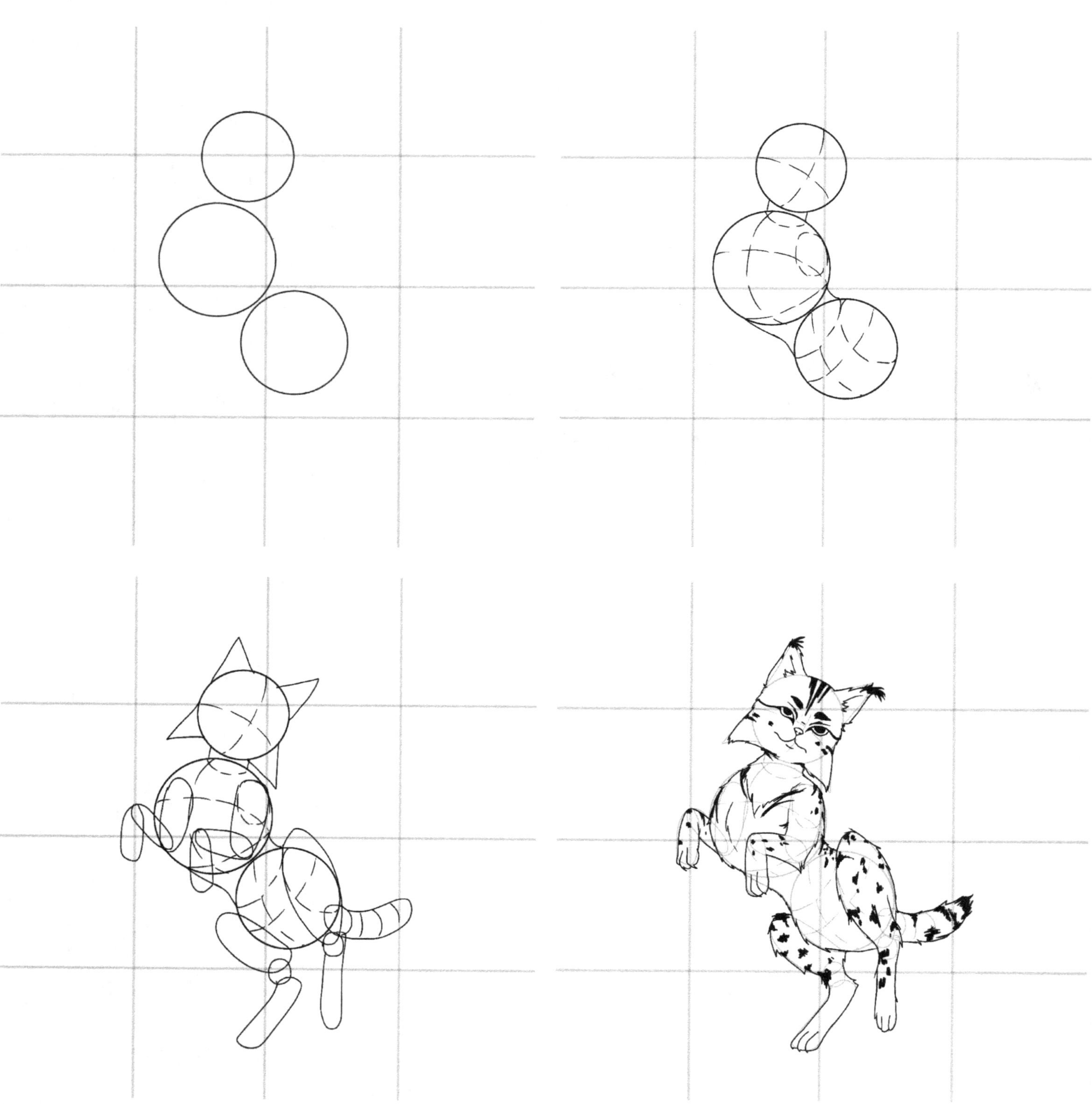

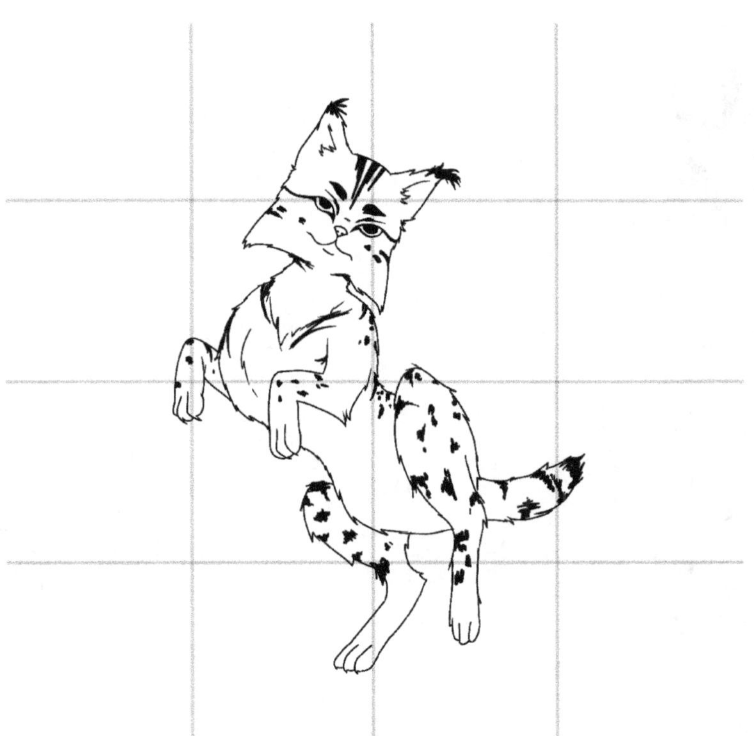

TRY IT HERE!

Lynx

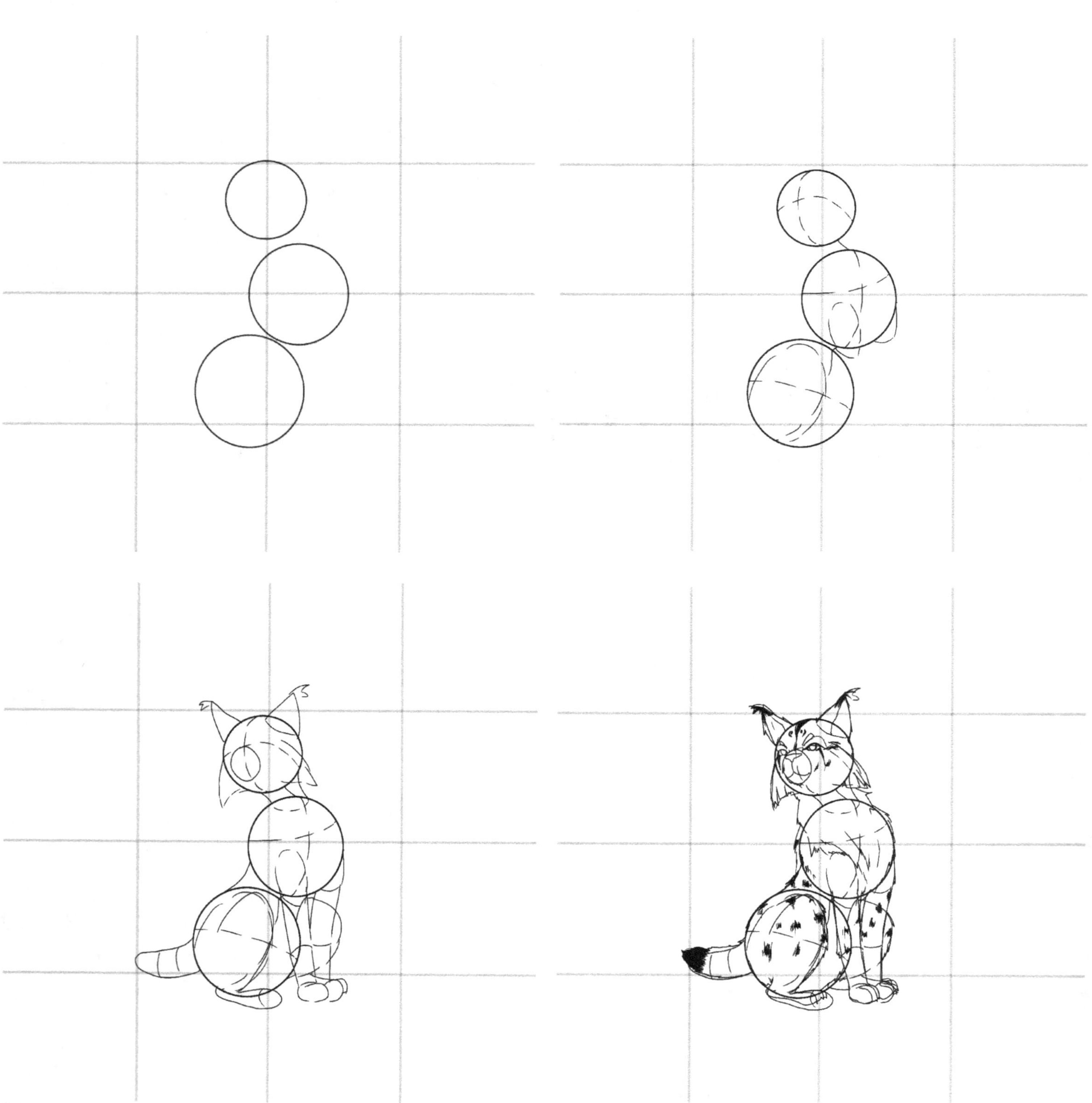

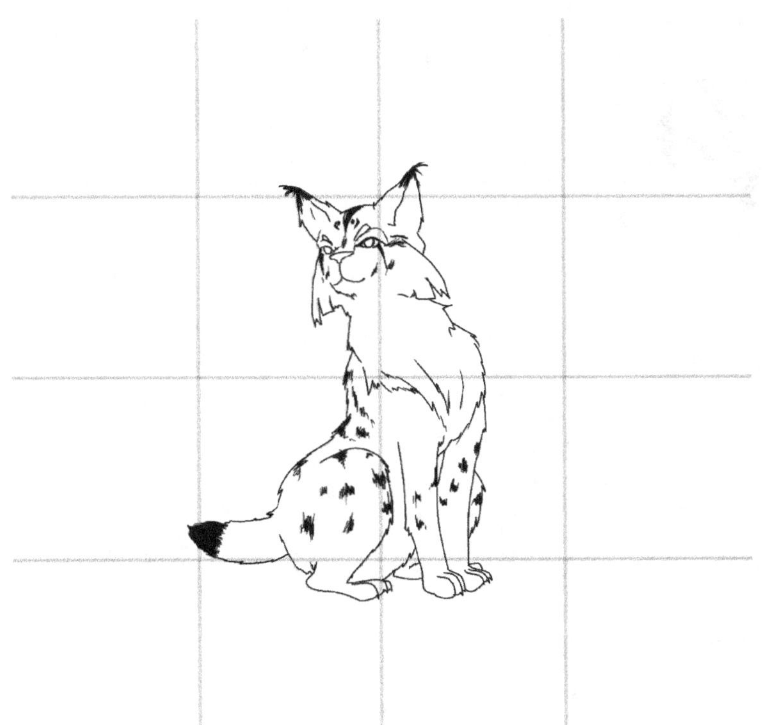

TRY iT HERE!

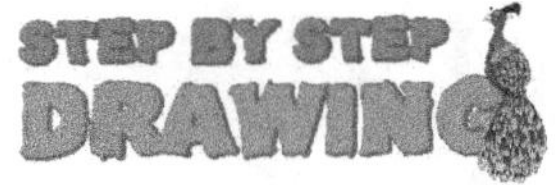

OKAPI

TRY IT HERE!

ORANGUTAN

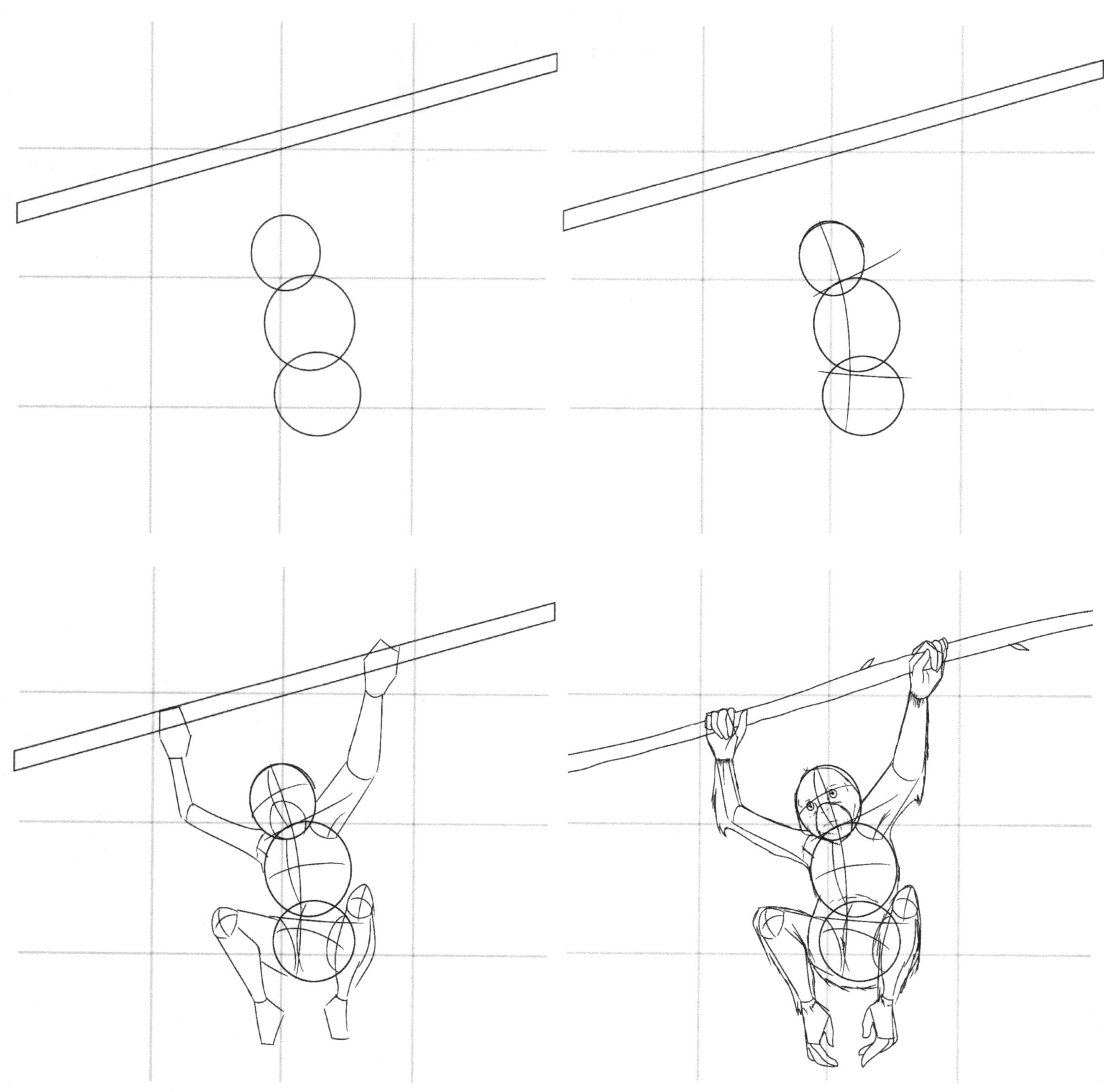

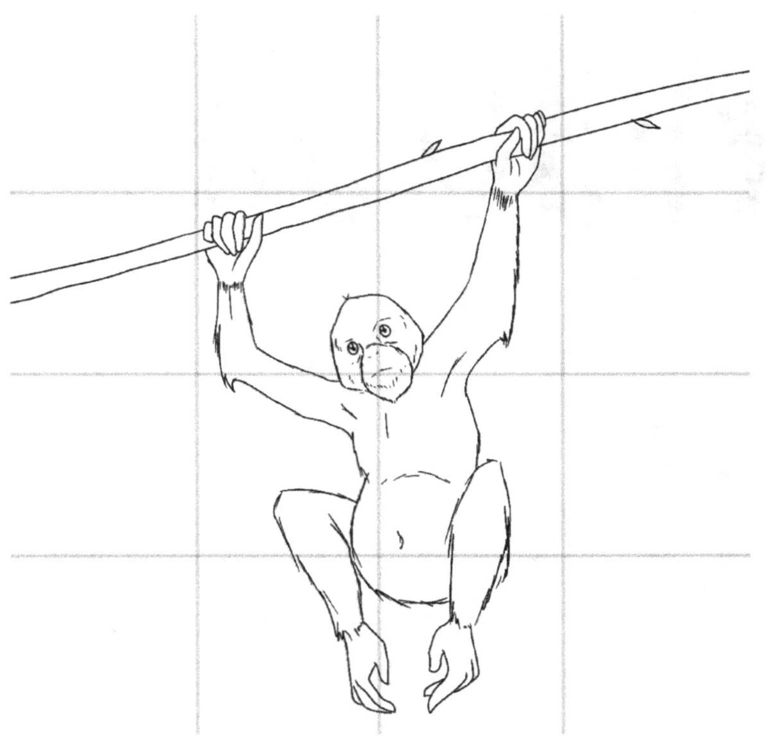

TRY it HERE!

ORANGUTAN

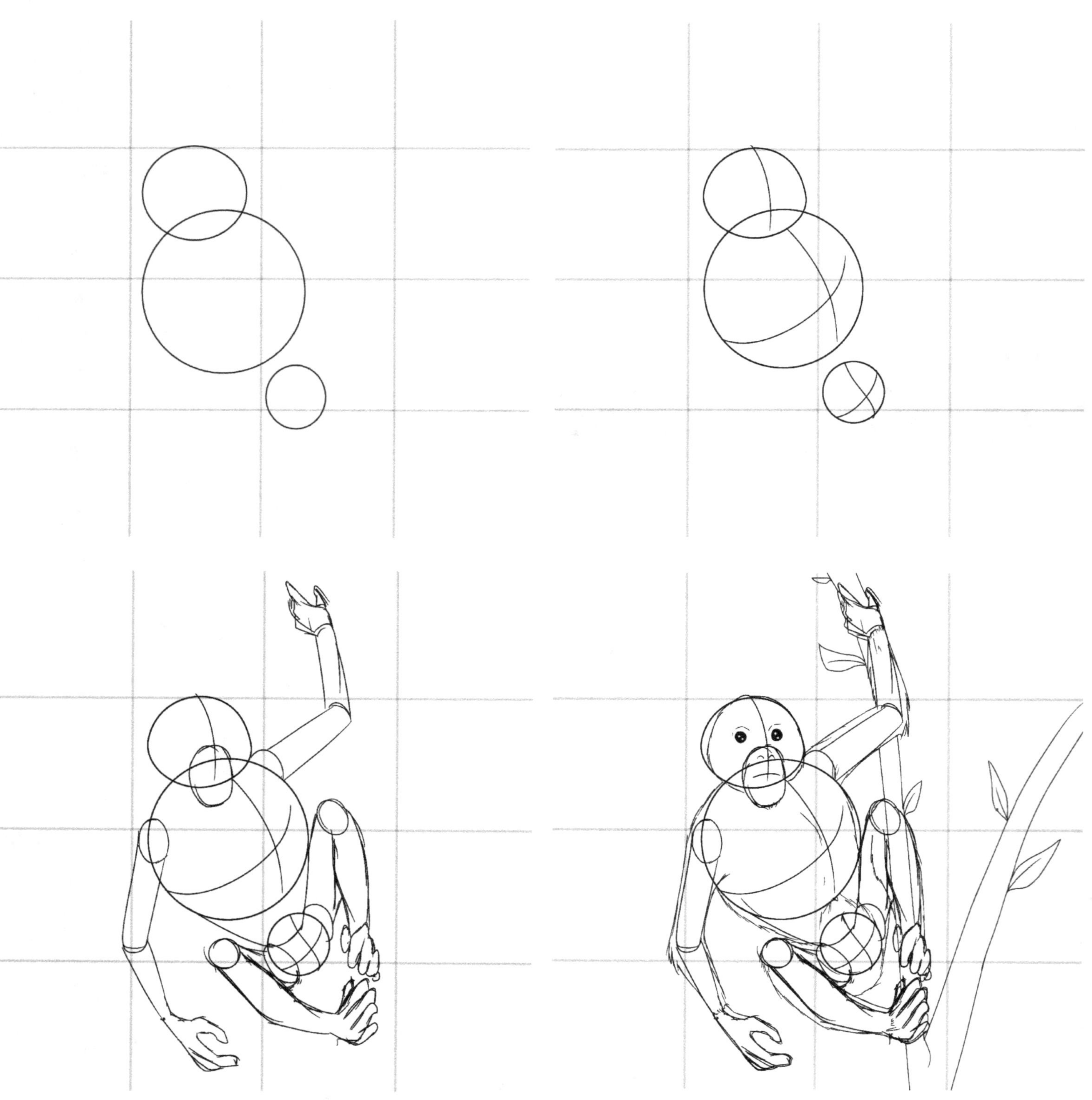

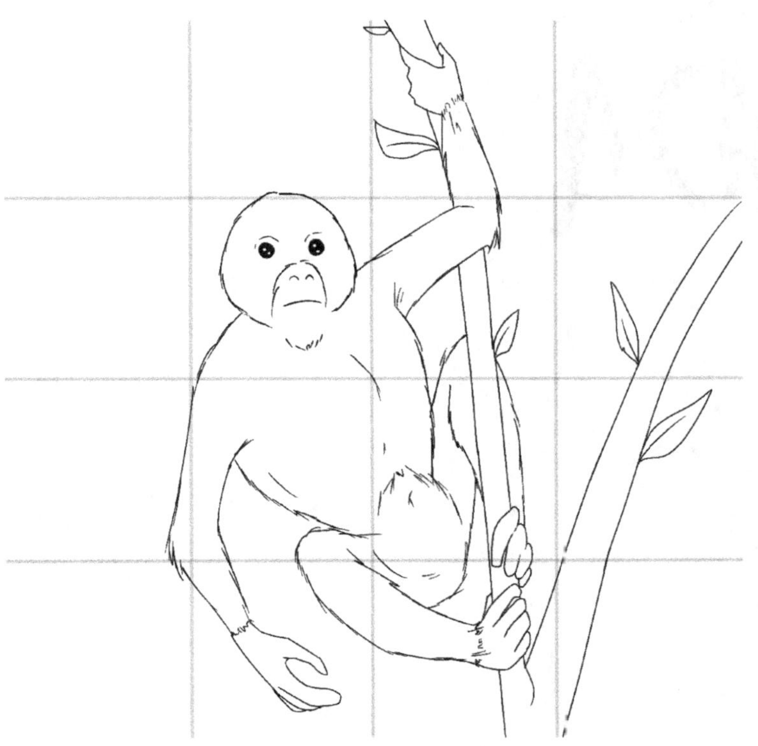

TRY iT HERE!

PANDA

TRY IT HERE!

PANDA

TRY iT HERE!

PANTHER

TRY IT HERE!

PANTHER

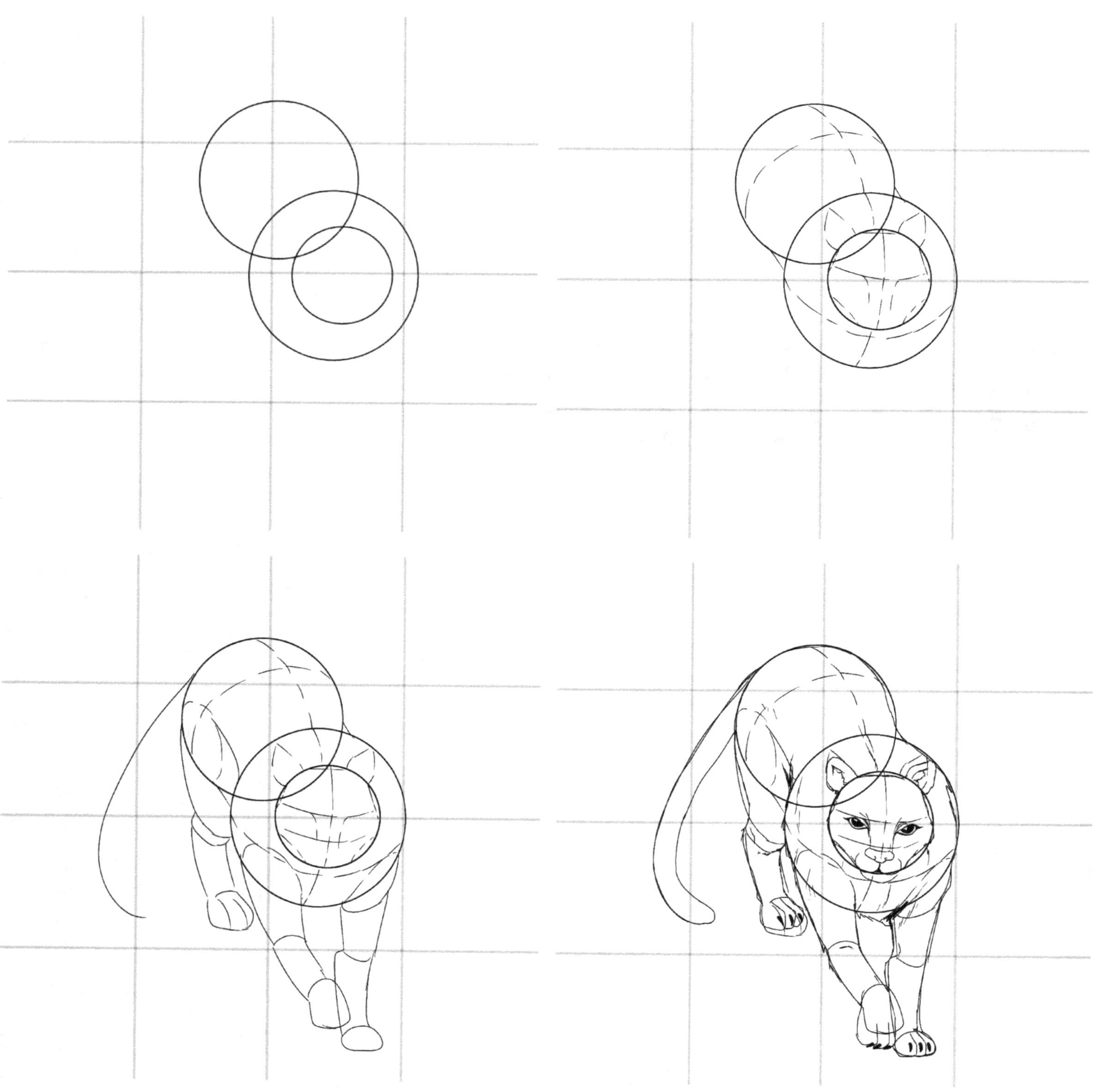

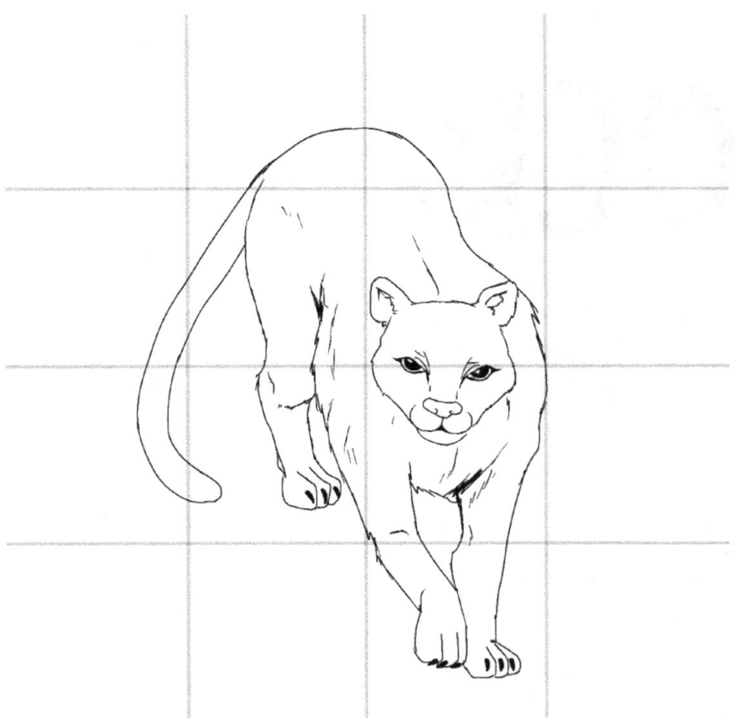

TRY it HERE!

PEACOCK

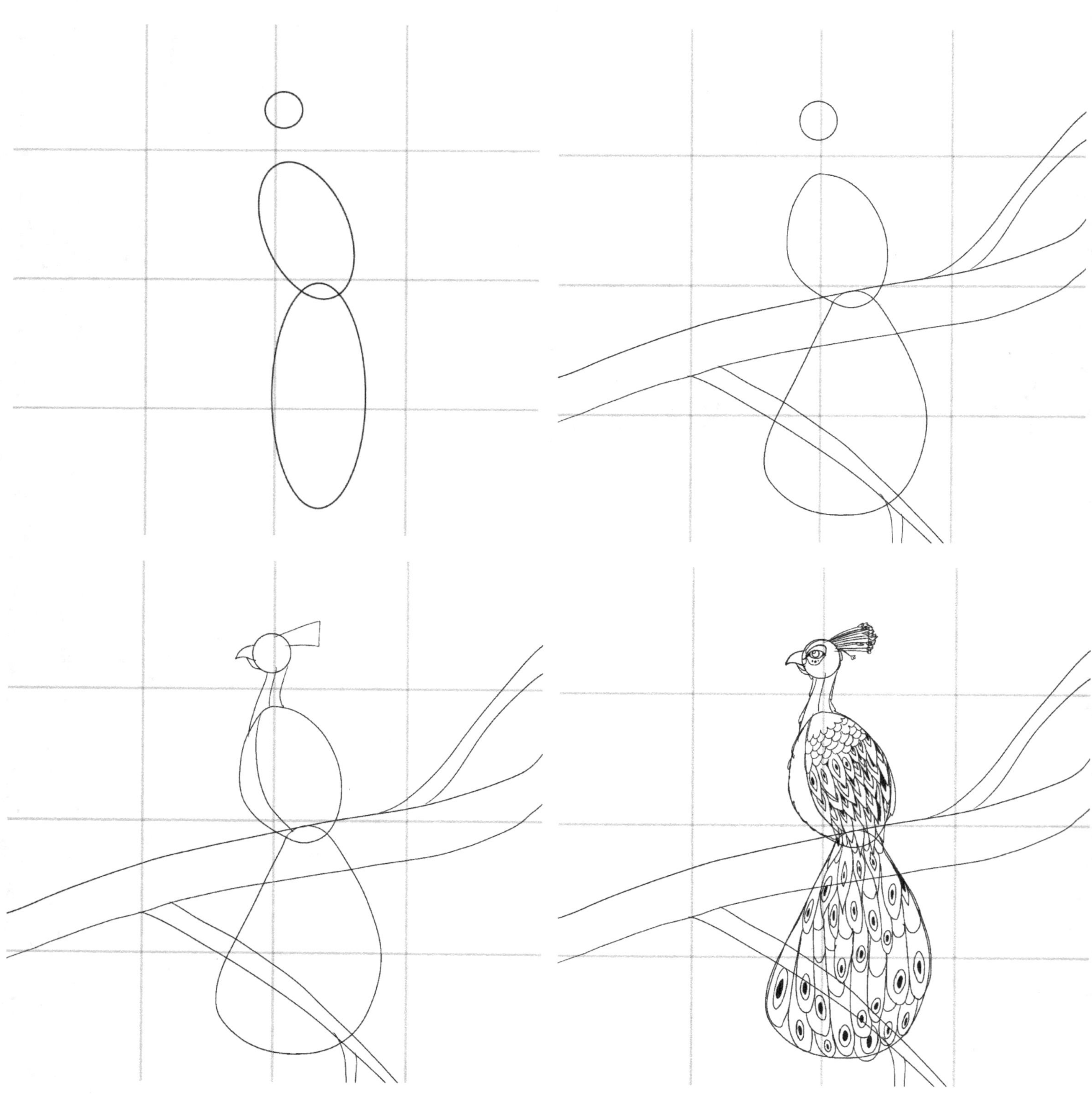

TRY iT HERE!

PEACOCK

TRY IT HERE!

PRAYING MANTIS

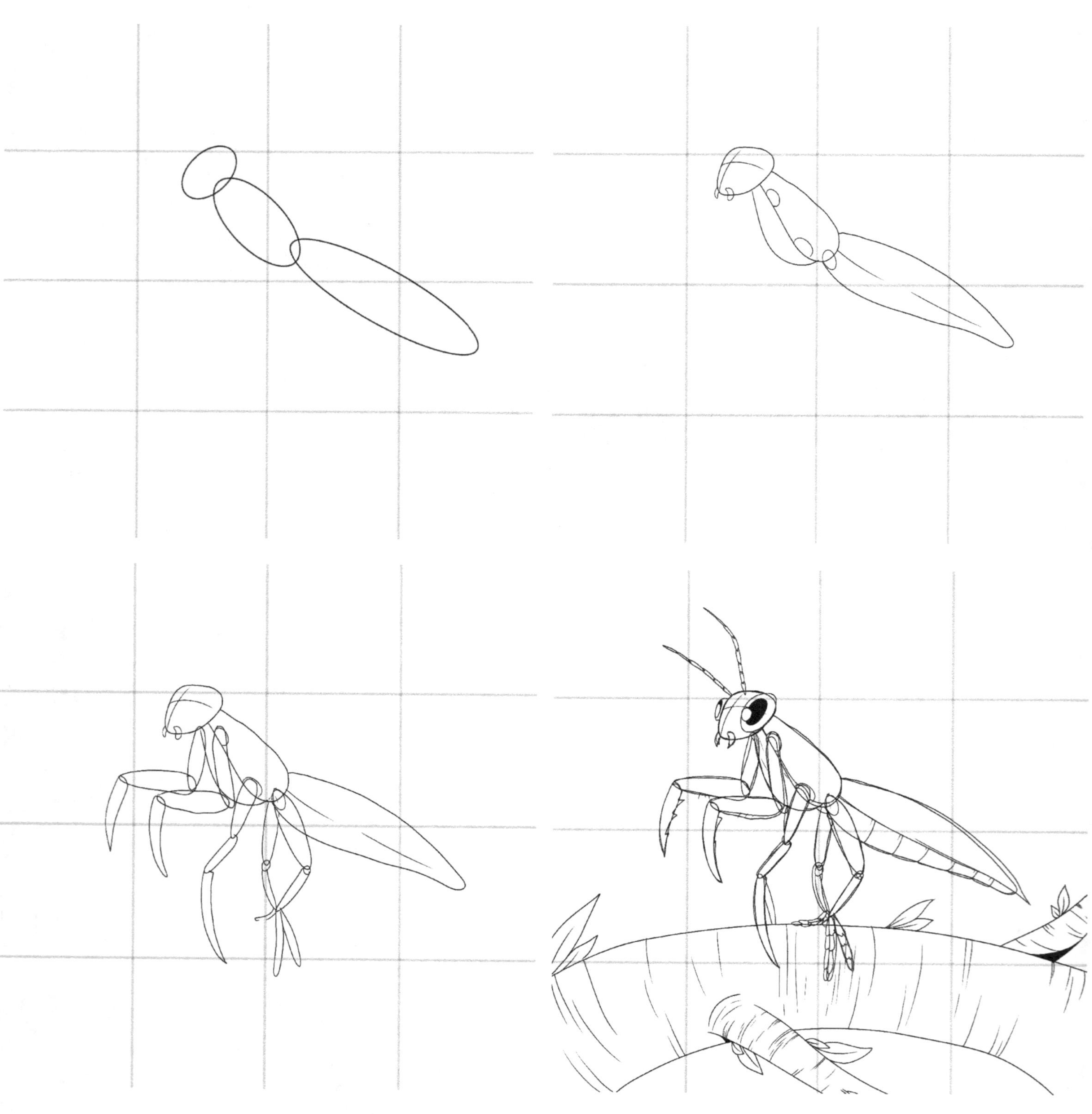

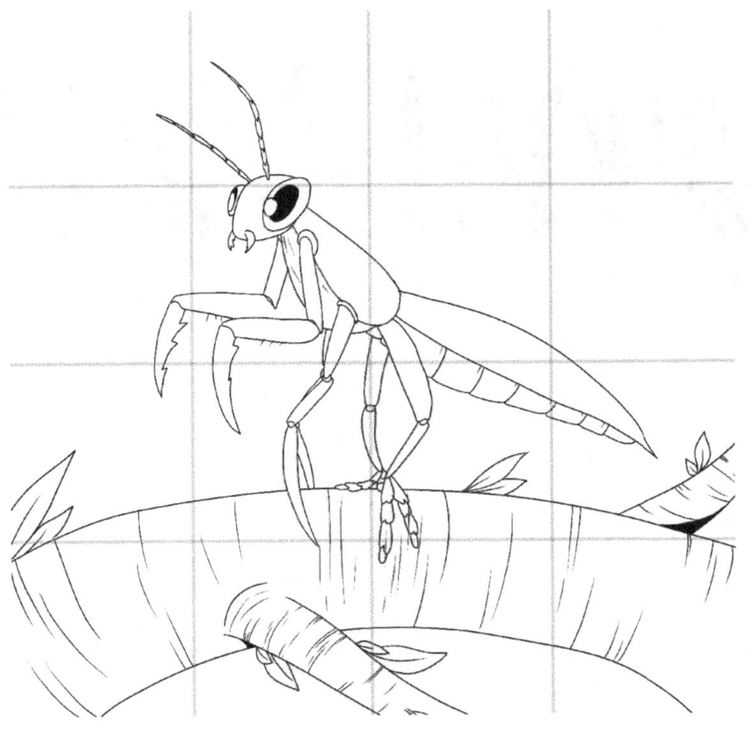

TRY iT HERE!

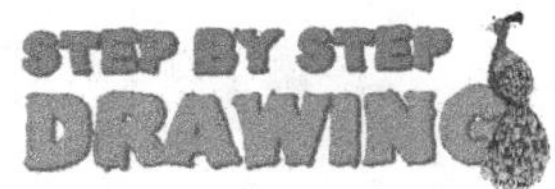

PRAYING MANTIS

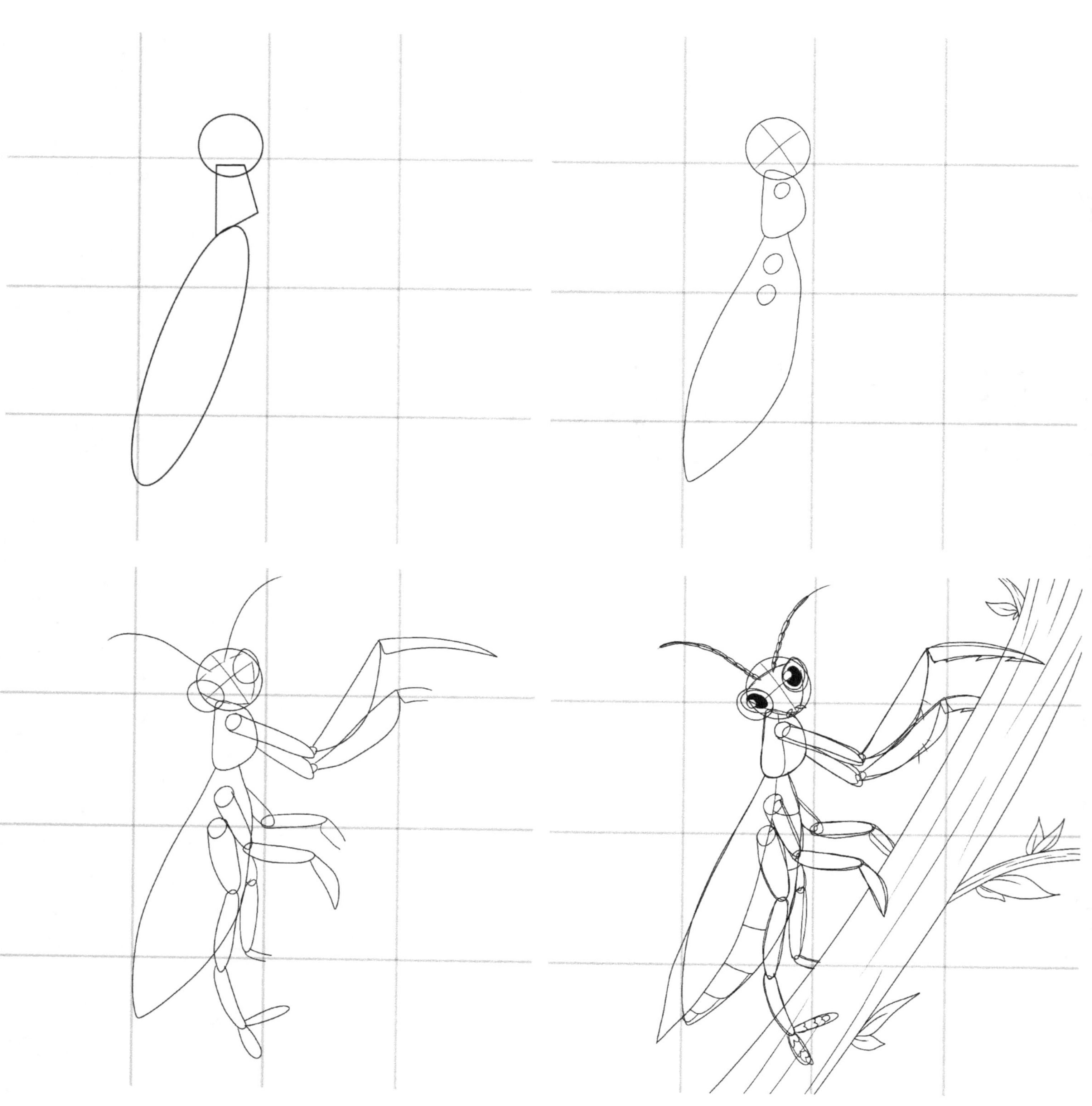

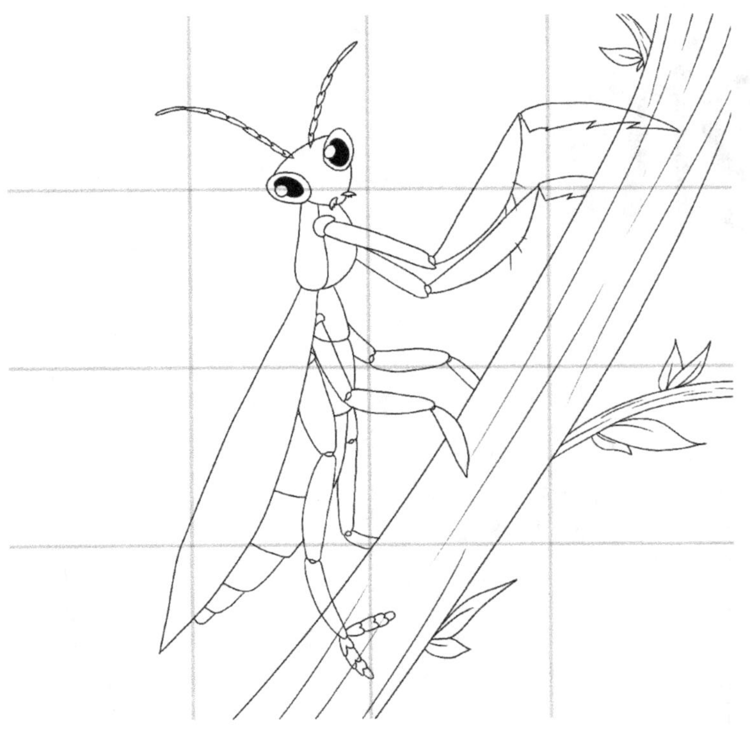

TRY IT HERE!

RABBIT

TRY iT HERE!

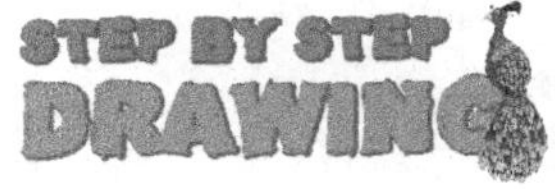

RABBIT

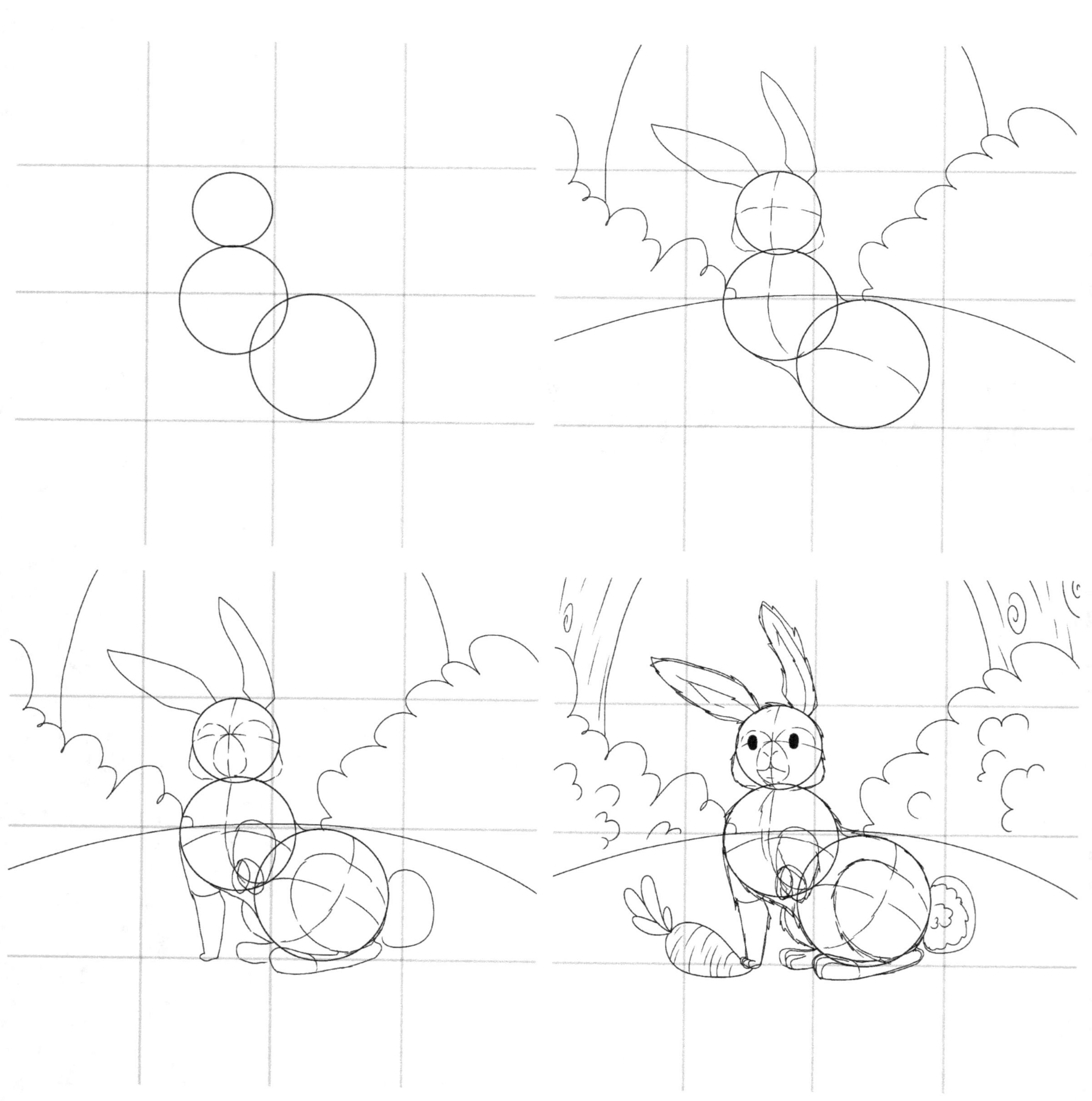

TRY IT HERE!

RACCOON

TRY iT HERE!

RACCOON

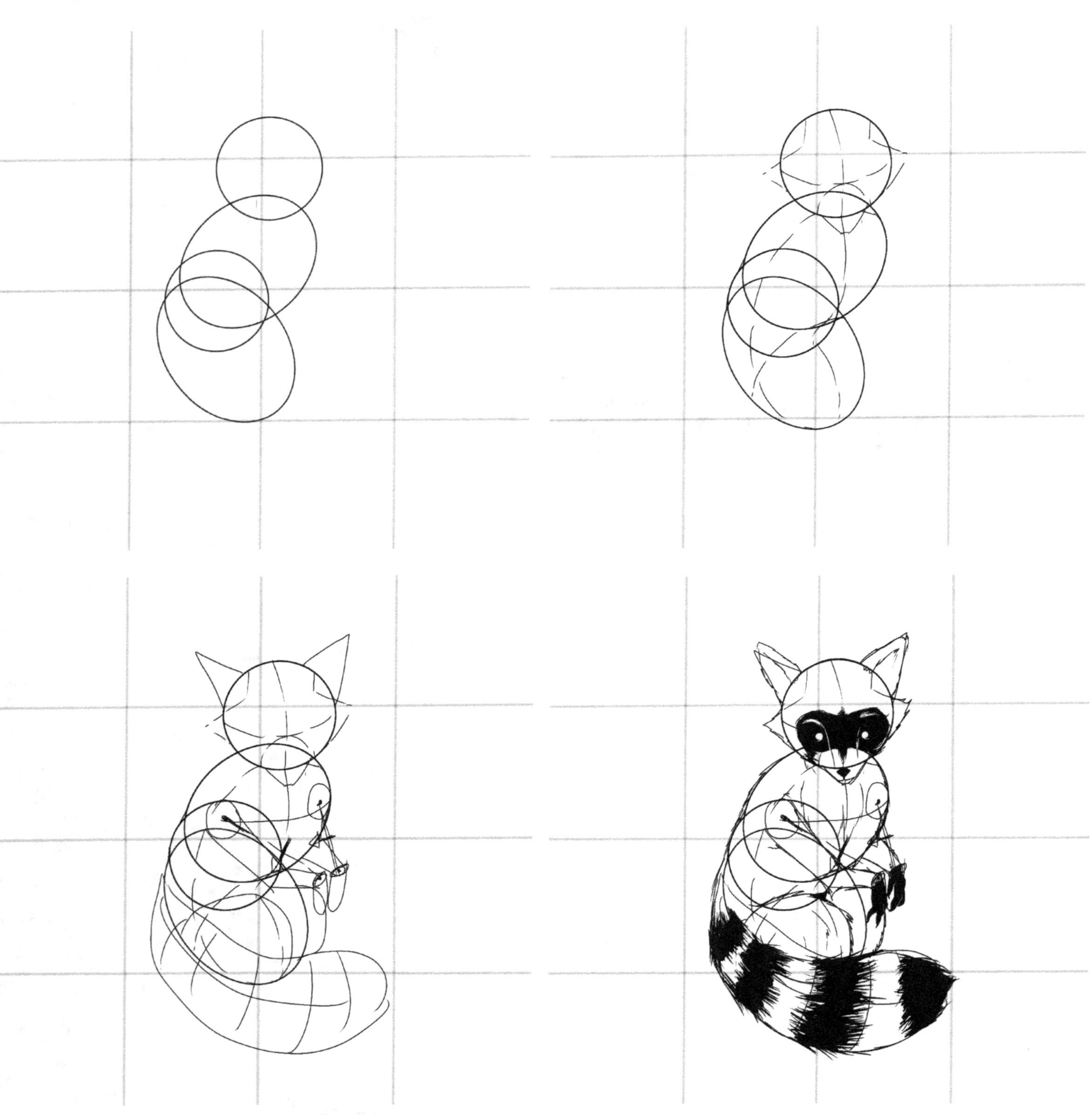

TRY it HERE!

RAMPHOCELUS

TRY it HERE!

TRY iT HERE!

SNAKE

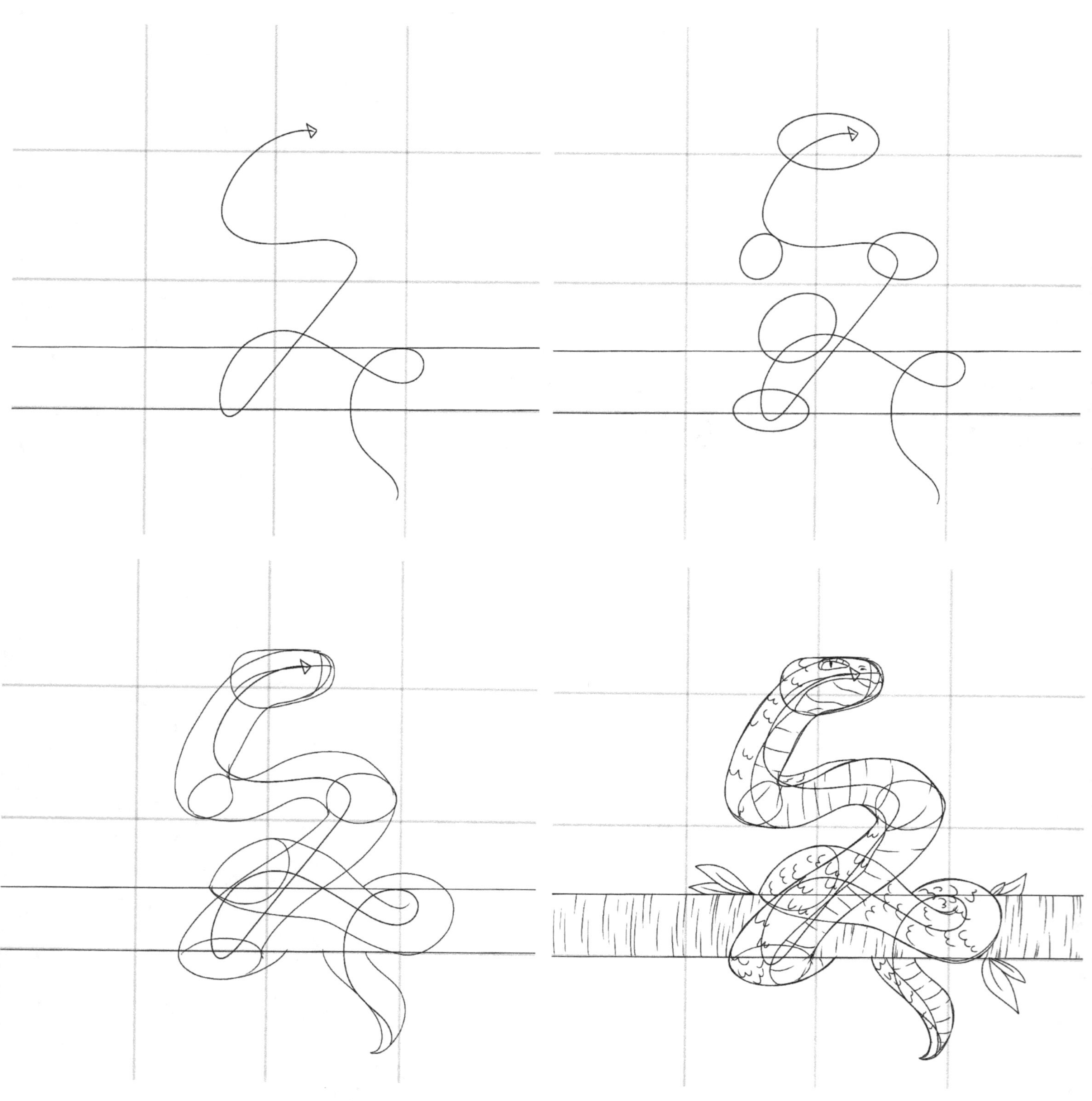

TRY IT HERE!

SNAKE

TRY IT HERE!

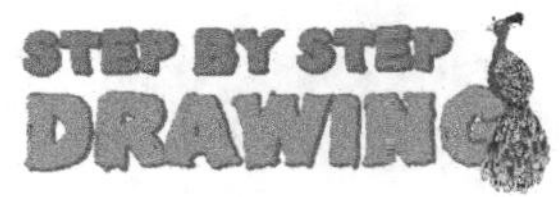

SQUIRREL

TRY iT HERE!

SQUIRREL

TRY IT HERE!

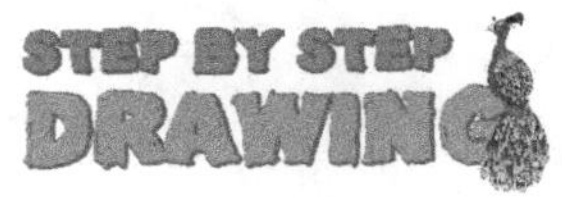

WILD PIG

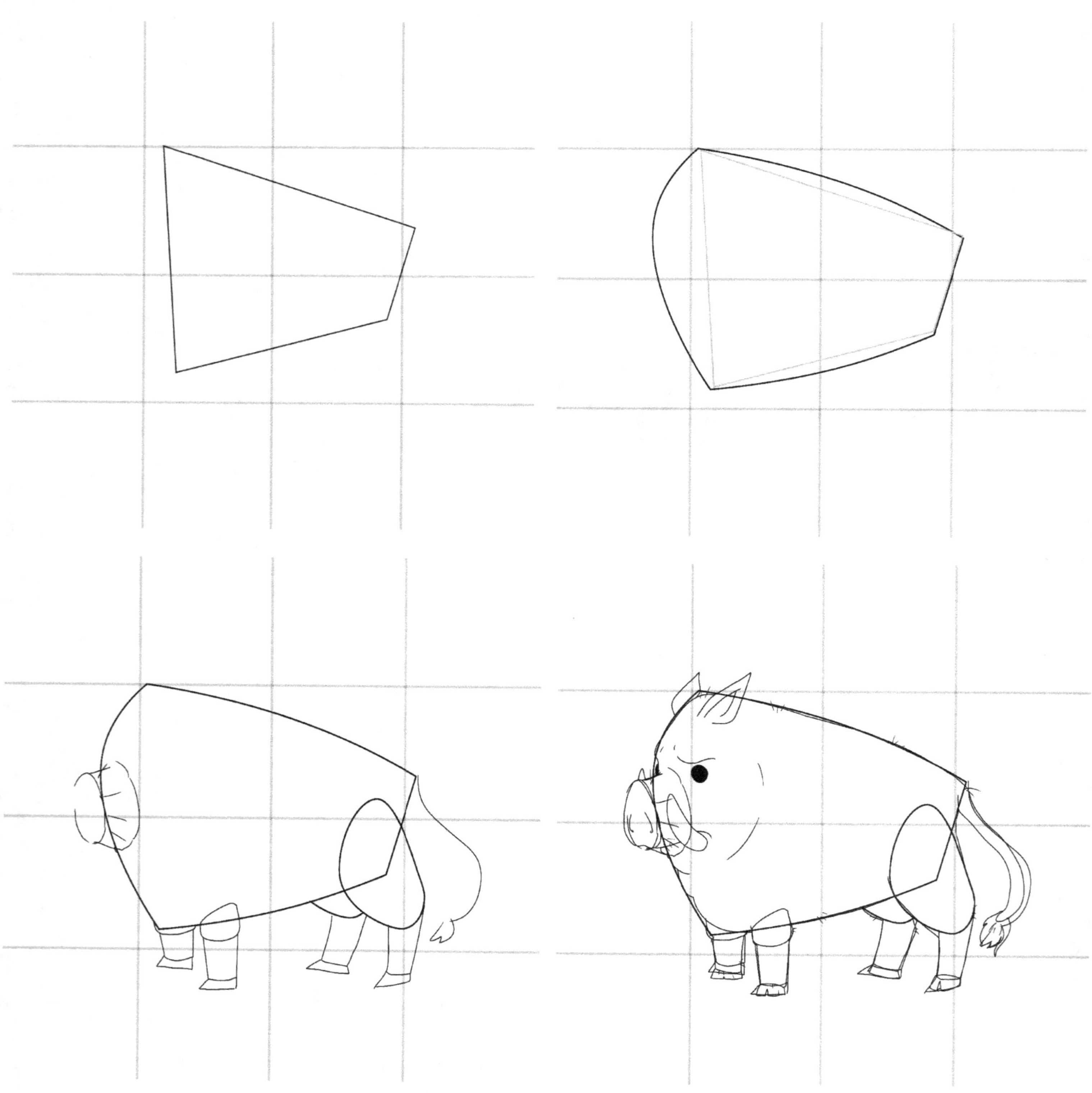

TRY it HERE!

WILD PIG

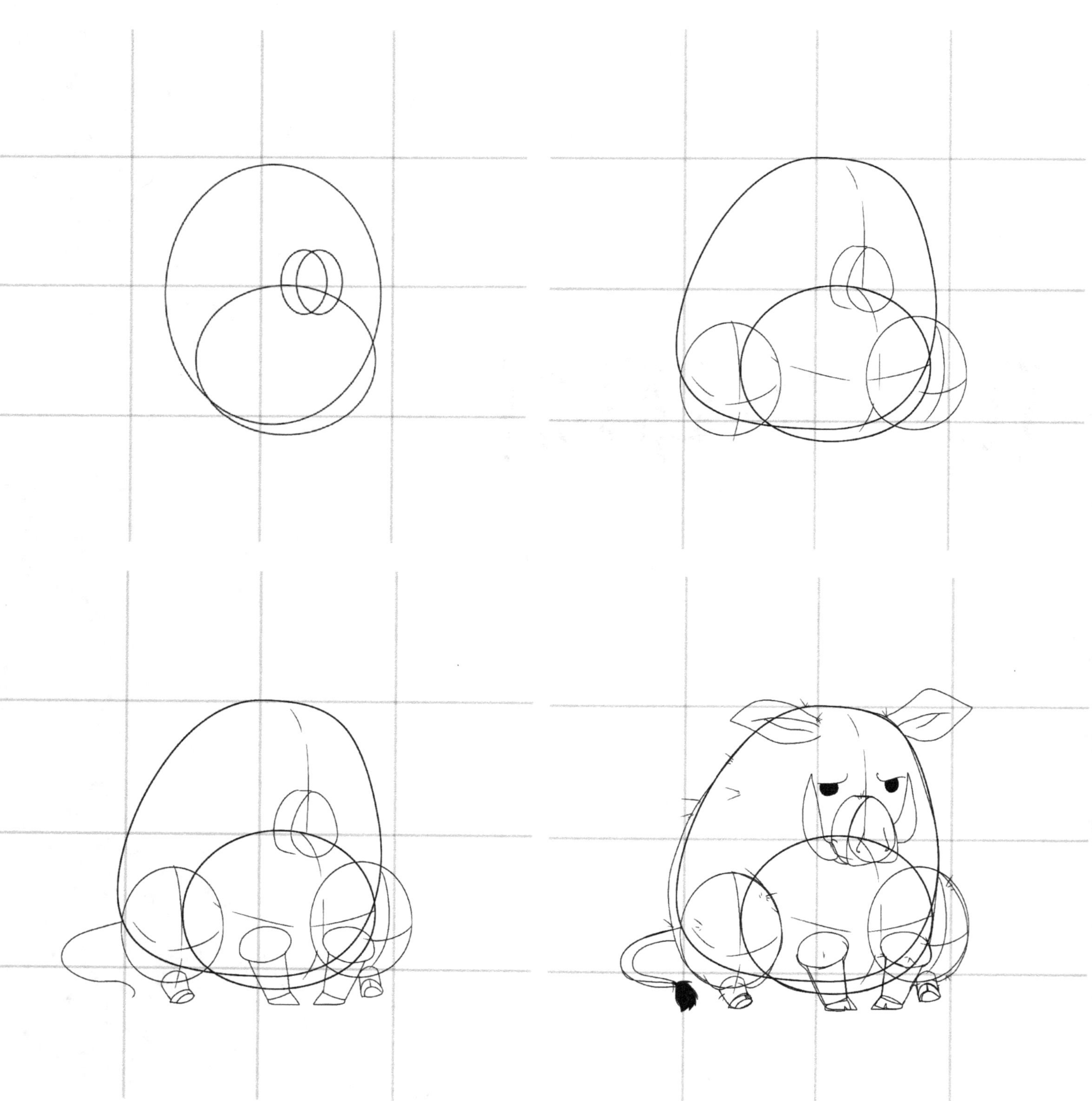

TRY IT HERE!

ACKNOWLEDGMENTS

A huge thank you to my family and to my friends, who inspire me daily with not only their art and great skills but with the perseverance and will to work the way they do, you are great artists, and I am lucky to call you all my friends.

A big thank you to every one of you that has given my book and myself the chance to guide you through this journey. The fact that you keep checking out my books makes me feel so special.
Practice and be patient with yourself and let your art speak through you.

If you have 20 seconds, please take a moment to leave a rating or review on Amazon, reviews really help us authors so much!

Did you like this book?

Be sure to check out the rest of

The Step by Step series by Little Pencil.

Keep practicing your awesome skills all the way from our wild Forest Animals to the depths of the Ocean, each with different difficulty levels!

littlepencilpress.com

Scan this code and get some FREE extras!

STEP BY STEP DRAWING